Creating Life-Long Learners

Creating Life-Long Learners

*Using Project-Based Management
to Teach 21st Century Skills*

Todd Stanley

CORWIN
A SAGE Company

A SAGE Company

FOR INFORMATION:

Corwin
A SAGE Company
2455 Teller Road
Thousand Oaks, California 91320
(800) 233-9936
www.corwin.com

SAGE Publications Ltd.
1 Oliver's Yard
55 City Road
London EC1Y 1SP
United Kingdom

SAGE Publications India Pvt. Ltd.
B 1/I 1 Mohan Cooperative Industrial Area
Mathura Road, New Delhi 110 044
India

SAGE Publications Asia-Pacific Pte. Ltd.
3 Church Street
#10-04 Samsung Hub
Singapore 049483

Printed in the United States of America

ISBN 978-1-4833-7719-3

This book is printed on acid-free paper.

Senior Acquisitions Editor: Jessica Allan
Senior Associate Editor: Kimberly Greenberg
Editorial Assistant: Cesar Reyes
Production Editor: Amy Schroller
Copy Editor: Lana Todorovic-Arndt
Typesetter: C&M Digitals (P) Ltd.
Proofreader: Jennifer Grubba
Indexer: Robie Grant
Cover Designer: Karine Hovsepian
Marketing Manager: Lisa Lysne

SFI Certified Sourcing
www.sfiprogram.org
SFI-00453

15 16 17 18 19 10 9 8 7 6 5 4 3 2 1

Table of Contents

Visit the companion website at
http://resources.corwin.com/StanleyCreatingLearners
for additional resources.

Acknowledgments

Corwin gratefully acknowledges the contributions of the following reviewers:

Marsha Basanda
Fifth-Grade Teacher
Monarch Elementary School
Simpsonville, SC

Polly BeeBout
Middle Science Teacher
CY Middle School
Casper, WY

Avis Canty-Duck
Special Education Teacher and
    Technology Facilitator
Greenville County Schools
Greenville, SC

Marcia Carlson
Sixth-Grade Teacher
Crestview Elementary School
Clive, IA

Tamara Daugherty
Art Teacher
Lakeville Elementary School
Apopka, FL

Elaine Ealy
Teacher/Adjunct Professor
Crestwood Middle School
Royal Palm Beach, FL

Katina Keener
Principal
Achilles Elementary
    School
Hayes, VA

Debra K. Las
Science Teacher
Rochester Public Schools,
    ISD#535
Rochester, MN

Darron Laughland
Special Education Teacher/
    Case Manager
Kennett High School
North Conway, NH

Laurie McDonald
Teacher
Duval County
    Schools
Jacksonville, FL

Cathy Patterson
Fifth-Grade Teacher;
    Former Assistant
    Principal
Walnut Valley USD
Walnut, CA

Michelle Tavenner
Sixth-Grade Teacher,
    Language Arts
Gahanna Middle School East
Gahanna, OH

Dr. Karen L. Tichy
Associate Superintendent for
    Instruction and Special
    Education
Archdiocese of St. Louis
St. Louis, MO

About the Author

 **Todd Stanley** is the author of seven teacher education books including *Project-Based Learning for Gifted Students: A Handbook for the 21st Century Classroom* and *Performance-Based Assessment for 21st Century Skills.* He has been a classroom teacher for the past 18 years and was a National Board Certified teacher. He helped create a gifted academy for Grades 5–8 where they employ inquiry-based learning, project-based learning, and performance-based assessment. He is currently a gifted intervention specialist for Reynoldsburg City Schools and lives in Pickerington, Ohio, with his wife Nicki and two daughters, Anna and Abby.

This book is dedicated to all the teachers
past and present from the Gateway Gifted Academy
who allowed me to grow as an educator and learn from the best.

Introduction—
Why Manage
Your Classroom

We need to prepare students for THEIR future not OUR past.

—Ian Jukes

There has been a push as of late in education to be teaching students what is termed *21st century skills.* You might ask why this sudden focus on 21st century skills given that we are well over a decade into the 21st century. According to Thomas Friedman and his similarly titled book, it is because the world is becoming flat, that is, the world is not the gigantic place it once was. It was not that long ago that in order to correspond with someone overseas cheaply you had to write him or her a letter. If you were lucky, you could exchange four to five pieces of correspondence in a single year. With the advent of increased communications technology, it is not unreasonable to be connected with someone from any part of the world cheaply in seconds.

A lot has changed in just the last 30 years in the global community, and yet how much has changed in the way we teach our students? If someone were to invent a time machine and travel back 30 years to a school, how much different would it look? Sure you might be surprised at a blackboard as opposed to the white boards in most modern classrooms, but the class would probably still be taught in the same fashion with the teacher standing at the front giving the students information they will be tested on later. Why don't we update our methods of teaching along with everything else that has advanced in the past 30 years? Because it is comfortable to teach in this manner. It is the way we were taught and is the way we have been taught for hundreds of years. "Why fix it if it ain't broke," as the saying goes. The problem is, recent statistics have shown, it may be broken.

Since we are on a more global playing field, it makes sense to compare students from the United States to students from other countries. So how does the United States stack up (Institute of Education Services, 2011)?

Math		
4th Grade Math	**8th Grade Math**	**12th Grade Math**
1. Singapore – 625	1. Singapore – 643	1. Netherlands – 560
2. Korea – 611	2. Korea – 607	2. Sweden – 552
3. Japan – 597	3. Japan – 605	3. Denmark – 547
4. Hong Kong – 587	4. Hong Kong – 588	4. Switzerland – 540
5. Netherlands – 577	5. Belgium – 565	5. Iceland – 534
6. Czech Republic – 567	6. Czech Republic – 564	6. Norway – 528
7. Austria – 559	7. Slovak Republic – 547	7. France – 523
8. Slovenia – 552	8. Switzerland – 545	8. New Zealand – 522
9. Ireland – 550	9. Netherlands – 541	9. Australia – 522
10. Hungary – 548	10. Slovenia – 541	10. Canada – 519
11. Australia – 546	11. Bulgaria – 540	11. Austria – 518
12. United States – 545	12. Austria – 539	12. Slovenia – 512
13. Canada – 532	13. France – 538	13. Germany – 495
14. Israel – 531	14. Hungary – 537	14. Hungary – 483
15. Latvia – 525	15. Russia – 535	15. Italy – 476
16. Scotland – 520	16. Australia – 530	16. Russia – 471
17. England – 513	17. Ireland – 527	17. Lithuania – 469
18. Cyprus – 502	18. Canada – 527	18. Czech Republic – 466
19. Norway – 502	19. Belgium – 526	**19. United States – 461**
20. New Zealand – 499	**28. United States – 500**	20. Cyprus – 446
Grade Average – 529	Grade Average – 513	Grade Average – 500

Source: Trends in International Mathematics and Science Study (TIMSS), 2011.

According to the Trends in International Mathematics and Science Study (TIMSS, 2011), not so good in mathematics. We are 28th with our eighth graders and near the bottom of the list for twelfth grade. In both, we are below the international average.

Science results are not much better (Institute of Education Services, 2011).

We start strong in the fourth grade but then fade fast, becoming below average by the twelfth grade. Some would argue this is because we have

Science		
4th Grade Science	**8th Grade Science**	**12th Grade Science**
1. Korea – 597	1. Singapore – 607	1. Sweden – 559
2. Japan - 574	2. Czech Republic – 574	2. Netherlands – 558
3. United States – 565	3. Japan – 571	3. Iceland – 549
4. Austria – 565	4. Korea – 565	4. Norway – 544
5. Australia – 562	5. Bulgaria – 565	5. Canada – 532
6. Netherlands – 557	6. Netherlands – 560	6. New Zealand – 529
7. Czech Republic – 557	7. Slovenia – 560	7. Australia – 527
8. England – 551	8. Austria – 558	8. Switzerland – 523
9. Canada – 549	9. Hungary – 554	9. Austria – 520
10. Singapore – 547	10. England – 552	10. Slovenia – 517
11. Slovenia – 539	11. Belgium – 550	11. Denmark – 509
12. Ireland – 539	12. Australia – 545	12. Germany – 497
13. Scotland – 536	13. Slovak Republic – 544	13. France – 487
14. Hong Kong – 533	14. Russia – 538	14. Czech Republic – 487
15. Hungary – 531	15. Ireland – 538	15. Russia – 481
16. New Zealand – 531	16. Sweden – 535	**16. United States – 480**
17. Norway – 530	**17. United States – 534**	17. Italy – 475
18. Latvia – 512	18. Germany – 531	18. Hungary – 471
19. Israel – 505	19. Canada – 531	19. Lithuania – 461
20. Iceland – 505	20. Norway – 527	20. Cyprus – 448
Grade Average – 524	Grade Average – 516	Grade Average – 500

Source: Trends in International Mathematics and Science Study (TIMSS), 2011.

such a large population and a policy of No Child Left Behind, while other countries test only their best and brightest. If that is indeed the case, we should compare the data using only our top students. Then it might tell a different story (Institute of Education Services, 2011).

Grade 12 Top Students	
Grade 12 Advanced Math	**Grade 12 Advanced Science**
1. France – 557	1. Norway – 581
2. Russia – 542	2. Sweden – 573
3. Switzerland – 533	3. Russia – 545
4. Australia – 522	4. Denmark – 534
5. Denmark – 522	5. Slovenia – 523
6. Cyprus – 518	6. Germany – 522
7. Lithuania – 516	7. Australia – 518
8. Greece – 513	8. Cyprus – 494
9. Sweden – 512	9. Latvia – 488
10. Canada – 509	10. Switzerland – 488
11. Slovenia – 475	11. Greece – 486
12. Italy – 474	12. Canada – 485
13. Czech Republic – 469	13. France– 466
14. Germany – 465	14. Czech Republic – 451
15. **United States – 442**	15. Austria – 435
16. Austria – 436	16. **United States – 423**
Grade Average – 501	Grade Average – 501

Source: Trends in International Mathematics and Science Study (TIMSS), 2011.

As you can see, the story remains the same. A twelfth grader in the United States is still below average in both advanced science and math.

How do we better prepare our students to compete in the global economy? Should we better train them for specific jobs? Unfortunately, that is not the answer. In Linda Darling-Hammond's book *The Flat World and Education* (2013), she points out that "the top 10 in-demand jobs projected for 2010 did not exist in 2004" (p. 2). That means schools have the difficult task of preparing students for jobs that do not even exist yet.

How does one do that? By teaching skills that would apply to any job. That is why you manage your classroom rather than teach it. If you manage students to think for themselves, be creative, problem solve, and take responsibility, you are teaching them a skillset that would be valued in the business world and translate to almost any position. Darling-Hammond describes the ideal 21st century skills classroom as one that would "enable students to learn how to learn, create, and invent the new world they are entering" (p. 3). That is why you manage your classroom: to create such students.

The business world is calling for these 21st century students. They are looking for a particular skillset that the traditional classroom might not be preparing them for. Clay Parker, CEO of BOC Edwards Chemical Management Division has stated,

> Our business is changing, and so the skills our engineers need change rapidly, as well. We can teach them the technical stuff. But for employees to solve problems or to learn new things, they have to know what questions to ask. And we can't teach them how to ask good questions— how to think.

> (Wagner, 2008, p. 2)

Ted McCain and Ian Jukes add to this when they say,

> In the good old days, what you learned in your youth prepared you for your single career. Today, learning has become a lifelong process. Given the rapidly changing nature of our world, people of all ages must constantly learn and relearn what they need to know. What they learned yesterday may no longer be valid in tomorrow's world. Tomorrow they will have to learn again because today's information will already be out of date.

> (McCain, 2001, p. 89)

In short, the global community is looking for thinkers. That is why there needs to be a shift in the educational philosophy that dominates many of our schools. The traditional classroom is designed to create memorizers. These are students that can remember content long enough to be tested on it. But are students gaining enduring understanding? Are they able to think and adapt the content to fit their needs? Traditional classrooms are designed to teach content, not skills such as thinking. Should we not be focusing more intently on skills so that we can create the thinking student that Darling-Hammond envisions?

This book will help you to manage your classroom so that your students become life-long learners who gain an enduring understanding through these 21st century skills. Not only will this make your students better thinkers, but it will also make you a better teacher. Each chapter will show you what this process of managing your classroom looks like and strategies for employing it. Chapter 1 explains what it means to manage your classroom and the advantages of doing so. Chapter 2 goes over the valuable 21st century survival skills that can be taught using this method that will better prepare students for the real world. Chapter 3 explains how to set it up, providing concrete examples for how this can be used in the classroom. Because teachers and students are accountable for the content standards in any given subject, it is important to center projects around these, and Chapter 4 shows how to do this. In order for this type of classroom to work, students must learn to work in groups and collaborate. This does not just happen, so Chapter 5 will provide strategies for guiding students through successful work in groups. Chapter 6 looks at risk management and how to prevent problems before they even happen. Chapter 7 looks at some different types of products that can be produced, while Chapter 8 discusses how to assess these products. Chapter 9 will talk about orienting the students as well as the teacher's role in the managed classroom and how it looks different than the traditional role teachers usually play. The afterward will wrap it all up and remind you of the type of student you will be creating using this method, the 21st century student. In the appendix, you will find blank forms that will aid you in your journey to transforming your classroom.

It is an exciting time to be a teacher right now. With Common Core State Standards and the increase in school technology, we are advancing our students into the 21st century and beyond. The question you have to ask yourself is, are you going to join them, or remain in the past?

Advantages to Managing Your Classroom

The difference between school and life? In school, you're taught a lesson and then given a test. In life, you're given a test that teaches you the lesson.

—Tom Bodett

Managing your classroom is not the same as *classroom management.* Classroom management is a discipline tool. It is making sure the lesson is organized and prepared to be given to students in a timely manner, that there is not much downtime between activities, and that students are quickly redirected when they get off task. Doing these things helps to ensure that students stay focused so they do not cause discipline problems. This skill is very valuable in a teacher and is a cornerstone to an effective classroom. Managing your classroom though is something different. It is a philosophy of teaching. Managing your classroom is giving your students a task to undertake and then guiding them along the way to make sure they are producing the best work possible. The major difference in managing the classroom and the traditional classroom is when one manages the classroom, he or she is not giving students the content. The teacher is giving students the means to find and understand that content.

A good way to compare it is how in the business world a project manager fosters a project. According to Penny Lewis (n.d.), a project manager, there are five steps to project management:

1. Planning

2. Organizing

3. Implementing

4. Controlling

5. Closeout

You can use these same steps in managing the classroom. As the teacher, you start out by planning your project. This usually is where you ask yourself the question, What is it I want my students to learn? These are what are termed the learning objectives. Many times, these will be based upon the Common Core Standards. Once this is determined, the project must be organized. Things to consider are due dates, product, audience, resources, and others. Some of this can be determined by the teacher or can be left up to the students. It all depends if there are particular skills the teacher wants students to learn. For instance, if the teacher wants students to demonstrate how to put together an electronic portfolio, the teacher would want to make that the product of the project. If not, the teacher might give the students some choice in what product they use to demonstrate what they have learned.

Another large difference between the traditional classroom and the one managed in the project management style of teaching is that the planning and organizing are the most involving for the teacher. As he or she begins to implement it to the students, the teacher turns over a majority of the responsibility to the students. This is one of the largest advantages of managing your classroom; the impetus for learning falls onto the shoulders of the student, not the teacher. This is an advantage because this is where the learner is created. As students begin to track down information, synthesize it into whatever form they need it to take, and apply it to a product that shows what they learned, this is the process of learning how to learn. Not only that; you are also empowering students to think for themselves. This confidence to learn is invaluable and will create 21st century learners. The controlling and closeout steps of project management require a different form of teaching than the traditional classroom. This is where the management aspect comes into play. What this management looks like will be discussed in far more detail in later chapters.

THE 21ST CENTURY THREE *R*S

What are the advantages to managing your classroom in this style? They are many direct and ancillary advantages to undertaking such a pedagogy, but let us simplify it into the three *R*s. These are not your grandfather's *R*s of *reading, writing,* and *arithmetic*. These are the 21st century *R*s of *readiness, responsibility,* and *relevance,* first introduced in the book *Project-Based Learning for Gifted Students* (Stanley, 2011).

Readiness

The great thing about managing your classroom is that you are not determining the starting or ending point for a student project when it comes to their skills and content. The only starting and ending points you are providing might be related to time such as due dates. Instead, you are giving them a task to complete. At what level a student does this is determined by him. Student #1 may come to the project with a great amount of background information and skills. This student need not spend time gathering this information again. He can start the project at a much further spot than a student who does not have this background knowledge. This allows the student to go into much greater depth, exploring higher-level thinking that he can handle because of this background knowledge. Student #2 might be starting from scratch. She might spend the first part of the project learning and trying to understand the basics of the topic. Once she gets these, she might only be able to produce lower-level understanding in her product but nonetheless, she gains an enduring understanding. Even though both students worked on the same task, they were able to go to very different levels of learning based upon the readiness of the student. This prevents students from being held back as well as allows students who need more time to be able to take it. As the project manager, you would need to recognize at what point your student is entering into the process and guide and encourage them along the way to the appropriate level of learning.

The readiness allows for natural differentiation where a student can achieve at the level he or she is able to. Students are able to challenge themselves based upon their level of readiness. As the manager of this project, you may have to step in from time to time to push students to that next level if they are unable to do so on their own, but if students are motivated, they will be pushing themselves in most cases.

Responsibility

Responsibility is a big factor in turning your classroom into a project management one. How much responsibility should you be giving your students? If they are to learn, the brunt of the responsibility should be on their shoulders. This does not mean the responsibility for turning in homework or the responsibility of being good in class. This is the responsibility for learning, the responsibility of figuring out how to demonstrate what has been learned, and the responsibility of managing their time. These are lifelong skills that if a student becomes accomplished at them, he or she will find it easier to be successful in the 21st century world.

The advantage of this is that by giving students a majority of the responsibility, you are empowering them as learners. They no longer have to wait for the teacher to give them the lesson. Because they have figured out how to think and learn on their own, there are limitless possibilities. It also will help to create leaders. By giving students the responsibility, instead of waiting around for someone to tell them what to do, they will take the initiative themselves to move their project forward. And when they encounter a roadblock, they will learn the skills and coping mechanisms to overcome these. These are problem-solving skills that are highly valued in the 21st century world.

The most important benefit is that you are creating students that can think and make decisions for themselves. This gives them a huge advantage over students who are intelligent, but do not have these valuable skills.

Relevance

Relevance is paramount when teaching 21st century skills. The work students do must be relevant to the world as well as their lives. This does a couple of things. By being relevant to the world, it allows students to see the big picture and how things fit together. A lot of times, students learn content independent of one another and then have difficulty seeing how it fits together. Because of this, they are unable to apply it to real life later on when the chance presents itself. This is where the disconnect happens in the traditional classroom. If you connect what students are learning to the real world, then they can react to it accordingly when they see it. This is how 21st century workers who can think on their feet are created.

Being relevant to the student is also important. Students often ask, what does this have to do with me? Students do this not because they are self-centered or rude. It is because like most people, they do not want to have their time wasted. One way to ensure it is relevant to students is by giving them choices. Choices in how they research, what the product will be, how they are evaluated. If students have some say so in these, they will care more about it because they are taking more ownership. In the project management style of teaching, students are given more choices.

Combining relevance with higher level thinking is how you want to set up your projects in your project management classroom. One tool to help with this is the rigor/relevance framework (see Figure 1.1) developed by the International Center for Leadership in Education (Jones, 2006).

In this framework, you are looking to get students to a higher level of thinking on the Bloom's Taxonomy shown on the Y-axis, near the evaluation level. At the same time, you want to make relevant connections to the real world so you want to be at a 5 on the X-axis where they can apply to read world unpredictable situations. Ideally speaking, you want students to be in the domain D section of the chart. In that spot students would be thinking at a higher level, while making connections to the real world. This is what managing your classroom allows you to accomplish; students

Figure 1.1   Rigor/Relevance Framework

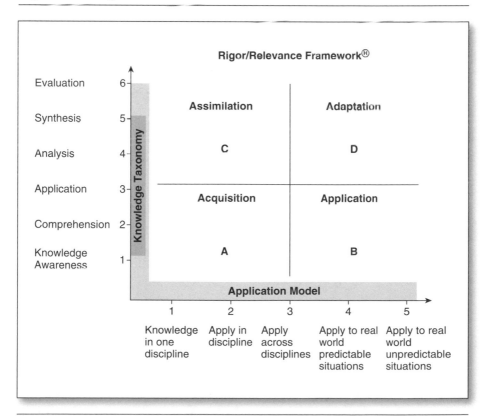

©International Center for Leadership in Education. Reprinted with permission.

working on projects that require a complexity of thinking in an authentic situation that links it to the real world. And because students are responsible for a lot of the decision-making process, they can make it relevant to their own lives by choosing things they care or are passionate about. This increases their level of motivation.

OTHER ADVANTAGES TO MANAGING YOUR CLASSROOM

The advantages to managing your classroom are very similar to those encountered when using project-based learning (PBL). According to the Buck Institute on Education, these

- Integrate curriculum areas, thematic instruction, and community issues
- Encourage the development of habits of mind associated with life-long learning, civic responsibility, and personal or career success.
- Overcome the dichotomy between knowledge and thinking, helping students to both "know" and "do"
- Assess performance on content and skills using criteria similar to those in the work world, thus encouraging accountability, goal setting, and improved performance
- Engage and motivate bored or indifferent students
- Support students in learning and practicing skills in problem solving, communication, and self-management
- Create positive communication and collaborative relationships among diverse groups of students
- Meet the needs of learners with varying skill levels and learning styles (Thomas, Mergendoller, & Michaelson, 1999)

Some of these advantages have already been addressed by the three Rs, but one that was not was the ability to integrate curriculum areas. Depending on how you set your projects up, you could have students integrate content from two or more subject areas, the advantage being of course that students see how all of the parts fit together in the real world. Many times, students are doing math in math class, science in science class. Seeing how these two work together in the real world takes the skill from being a practice to being something practical.

In addition, there is the idea of being able to communicate and collaborate successfully with others in a diverse group. Since you will be managing students in teams in a lot of cases, being able to work with others is a very important skill students will learn. This will translate into a valuable commodity for them in the professional world. How to foster these skills of communication and collaboration will be talked about at great length later in this book.

At Least Manage This

There is a lot to take in with regard to managing your classroom. At the end of each chapter, there will be a summary of the most important aspects of the chapter. This way, if you ever need to refresh your memory on how to manage your classroom, you can look back at this part as a trigger to do so.

Probably the biggest advantage that managing your classroom provides is that it creates 21st century thinkers. Thinkers are what the business world is looking for in a prospective employee. Empowering your students to make decisions and think for themselves will be a huge advantage for them when they are competing for positions in the global market.

Importance of 21st Century Skills

If we teach today's students as we taught yesterday's, we rob them of tomorrow.

—John Dewey

As the above quote so eloquently points out, students need to be prepared not for yesterday, not even for today, but for tomorrow. In order to do that, we need to make sure our classrooms are places where valuable skills, skills that enable students to function and thrive in the future world that awaits them, are taught. Many times in classrooms, we get bogged down with the content that can be very specific. How does a teacher ensure students will be prepared for the future if their future does not involve using the content being taught? The answer is to center the content around 21st century skills that are useful and that will translate into any profession. By doing that, not only are students learning the content, but they are gaining a skill that will be beneficial to them as well.

21ST CENTURY SURVIVAL SKILLS

Tony Wagner (2008) in his book *The Global Achievement Gap* mentions seven survival skills every student should leave the classroom with if he or she is going to compete in the global marketplace, all which can be taught in a PBL classroom very effectively:

1. Accessing and analyzing information

2. Curiosity and imagination

3. Initiative and entrepreneurialism

4. Adaptability

5. Effective oral and written communication

6. Critical thinking and problem solving

7. Collaboration across networks

Each of these by themselves cannot create a 21st century learner, but the combination of them used in your project-based learning (PBL) classroom will. In order to understand these skills better, we should define what each skill means, what the skill involves, how PBL can successfully teach it, and why it will be important in managing your students.

ACCESSING AND ANALYZING INFORMATION

Being able to access and analyze information comes down to the skill of information literacy. Trilling and Fadel (2009) define information literacy as the ability to

- Access information efficiently and effectively
- Evaluate information critically and competently
- Use information accurately and creatively (p. 65)

Like all 21st century survival skills, it is not just a skill for the classroom, it is a skill for life. Being able to figure out where to access information efficiently and effectively would be very important if you are trying to gain directions to a place you have never been before. Being able to evaluate information both critically and competently would come in handy when trying to discern which car you should buy. Using information accurately and creatively would certainly be beneficial if you have to find out how to put together your child's Christmas toy when the directions become lost. This skill transcends the classroom, so being able to perform it with a certain level of competence and confidence would make that person a valuable worker. Any time you are doing purposeful research in the classroom, this is a skill that will be taught. This research can come in the form of print or electronic resources.

When you use PBL in the classroom, students will often need to use information literary in order to complete an assignment. Research papers, lesson presentations, portfolios, and debates are just a few types of products that would require the skill of information literacy. Many times, teachers assume students have already been taught the skill of information literacy, especially if you have older students. This is a skill that must be retaught often. Students may have developed some bad habits, so going over the basics of how to conduct proper information literacy could be helpful to students at any level. Making sure students have an understanding of how to properly research both print and electronic is not something you should take for granted.

When working with students using literacy skills, you should cover the basics of how to conduct proper research. For example, if students are required to use the Internet to find information, teaching them

- how to craft a search using key words,
- which search engines will get them what,
- how to determine whether a website can be trusted or not, and
- how to synthesize information in their own words and properly cite the source so that they do not plagiarize

would all be building a good foundation for successful information literacy. The more experience students get with information literacy, the better they are going to become at it. As the project manager, you need to make sure this exposure is guided so the experiences students are having develop good practices rather than bad habits. Before beginning any project that involves information literacy, you might want to conduct a workshop or a brief presentation on how to use such a skill.

CURIOSITY AND IMAGINATION

The ability to generate ideas leads to the skill of curiosity and imagination. The more comfortable students get with thinking critically (or outside of the box thinking) the more imaginative their ideas are going to be. Although certain people are born being more imaginative than others, it is something that can be fostered and taught. If classrooms focus too heavily on facts, recall, simple skills, and test taking, students will not be ready to think imaginatively in the real world. As Sir Kenneth Robinson, a thought leader on creativity explained,

> Traditional education's focus . . . has not been good for the development of creativity and innovation. This is changing in the 21st century, and education systems from Finland to Singapore are beginning to put creativity and innovation as a high priority in their desired outcomes for student learning. (Trilling & Fadel, 2009, p. 57)

We need to come up with ways for students to use their curiosity and imagination in the classroom. The solution to this is in the products that you allow students to create for their projects.

PBL and the products they allow students to create is an effective way to allow for this imagination. If students must write a song to teach how to use a particular math formula, they will certainly have to use their imagination. If you are having students design and create their own experiment based on their interests, this allows them to explore their curiosity. If students have to record an interview to teach about the book *To Kill a Mockingbird*, they are able to tap into their creativity with how they convey this through spoken word. If students must debate the merits of the city-states of Sparta and Athens by role-playing a person from that time period, they can be innovative in how they form their argument and then present it.

Providing students with choice allows for much curiosity and imagination. Instead of prescribing the product, a project manager can allow students to come up with their own products. The more choices we give students, the more chances they have to be creative and innovative.

INITIATIVE

In the managed classroom, students are given a task, they are provided with resources to accomplish this task, and they are given a timeline by which they must have the task completed. Other than that, students are directing a lot of what they are doing themselves. Projects such as these require a good amount of self-direction and initiative. There is much choice provided, and students are the ones who determine how they are learning. There are many benefits to this approach, one explained here: "When individuals feel more like origins than pawns, they have higher self-esteem, feel more competent, and perform at higher levels of accomplishment" (Ryan & Grolnick, 1986, p. 550).

The project manager's role is to guide from the side, providing resources and guidance when needed, but otherwise to allow the students the space to direct themselves. This is how they will learn to be life-long learners, learners who do not need the carrot of a grade or assignment; someone who is a self-directed learner and takes initiative.

How valued would a person be to their employer if he or she takes initiative and does not need to be watched to make sure he or she is working? Would not you as the teacher want a classroom full of these students? You would be able to do what is every teacher's dream: teach. You would have the ability to move around the classroom and work with students individually, allowing them to grow to their potential rather than waiting for the common denominator of the class to catch up. When you provide students the freedom of self-directed learning, you get amazing results. Students are more motivated because they have choice in what it is they are doing rather than being directed. And students can be more imaginative because they are not constrained by as many requirements. They are getting into those higher levels of thinking you want students to achieve. Managing your classroom with PBL allows the teacher to put the impetus of learning on the student, where it should be.

Even though the students are directing most of their learning, there are certain resources you as the project manager can put into place that will help them to learn initiative. Three such resources are contracts, calendars, and rubrics. The purpose of a contract is to keep students focused on the task at hand. If you give them 3 weeks to work on a project, they may very well forget what the main purpose of the project is or what exactly their responsibilities are. The contract is a written reminder of what it is they are supposed to be doing. It lays out the goals and responsibilities that can be referred to whenever necessary (examples of blank contracts in the Reproducibles section). Students should complete the contract before they ever touch the project. This causes students to think about what they need or want to accomplish before they begin to work, making it more purposeful. Once the contract has been approved by the project manager/teacher and signed by all parties involved, students may begin the project. The contract can also be signed by the parents. This makes them aware of what their child is doing and be better able to help at home. Here is what a completed contract might look like:

PROJECT CONTRACT

Student Name: Ted

Project Name: Fort Perimeter

Time of Project: 2 weeks

Overall Goal of Project: To gain an understanding of what perimeter is and how it is used in everyday life

Learning Objectives:

- To learn what perimeter is
- Be able to determine the perimeter of objects based on the rules of perimeter
- To relate perimeter to the real life object of a tree fort

Product of Project: Create a drawing/model of a tree fort complete with a correct perimeter of the fort and how I arrived at this

The project manager will meet with students or groups periodically through a project. Each time all parties should check the contract to make sure they are living up to the agreement. Because the student created and agreed to the contract, he or she has ownership in what he or she is doing. The student has not let the teacher down when the project is not where it needs to be, but rather has let himself or herself, or his or her group mates down. This is part of learning responsibility that is a cornerstone of self-directedness and initiative.

To aid with the time management aspect, a good resource is the use of a calendar in which a student lists tasks and when they should be completed. Without these periodic deadlines, students may wait until the last moment to try and do everything. Whenever the project manager sits down to conference with a student/group it is helpful to look at the calendar to follow progress (blank calendars in the Reproducibles section). Here is an example of what a calendar might look like from the perimeter project:

Day 1	Day 2	Day 3	Day 4	Day 5
Gain an understanding of what perimeter is by reading Chapter 7 of the math book.	Get an idea of how to figure out perimeter by doing problems 1–25 on page 45 of Chapter 7.	Finish doing problems 1–25 on page 45 of Chapter 7.	Grade my work to be sure that I am doing it correctly/ look for examples in real life where perimeter would be used and why.	Brainstorm what my fort is going to be made of/ get the supplies needed for my fort.
Day 6	Day 7	Day 8	Day 9	Day 10
Create a plan of the fort and the dimensions of it.	Check the perimeter of the plan and make sure it is correct.	Begin to create the fort.	Continue to create the fort.	Check to make sure my plan and actual model match in perimeter/turn in the model of my fort.

This graphic organizer causes students to break the project into parts making it more manageable and helps them to see the steps necessary to complete the project.

The final piece of this initiative formula is the use of a rubric. The basic idea behind a rubric is the student determines the criteria for which he or she will be evaluated (or the teacher/project manager can provide one). This way, the student is completely aware of the expectations. This rubric is checked over and approved by the teacher just like the contract and calendar. The project manager would make sure the rubric measures what the student said he or she was going to learn in the contract. Students keep this rubric with them the entire project so they are clear on how they are going to be assessed on their performance. It acts as the blueprint for how to make an outstanding product (blank rubric in the Reproducibles section).

The combination of the contract, calendar, and rubric is a good method for teaching initiative in students. It allows them to learn the valuable skill of self-directedness.

ADAPTABILITY

Adaptability is one's ability to react to change. This is a valuable skill in the 21st century because we are developing technology at breakneck speed. It does not take more than a year or two to develop the newest technology that makes the old one obsolete. Those who are able to adapt to these changes often find much success. Those who are not able to keep up might find their skill set diminish. This is why doctors, lawyers, and teachers must continue learning throughout their careers, otherwise the techniques and procedures they use will become outdated. That is why adaptability is such an important skill to have in the real world.

How does one teach adaptability in the classroom though? PBL makes this quite easy to do. Trilling and Fadel (2009) suggest the following:

> The skills involved in flexibility and adaptability can be learned by working on progressively more complex projects that challenge student teams to change course when things aren't working well, adapt to new developments in the project, and incorporate new team members on both current and new projects.

> (p. 77)

In PBL, as the project manager, it is your job to set deadlines and to give a suggested timeline for when events should happen to help a student determine if he or she is behind. Even with this in place students must learn to manage their time within the framework of the deadline and adjust accordingly. For instance, say they have been given 2 weeks to conduct an analysis concerning the effectiveness of recycling in the community. The teacher/project manager has mapped out the following timeline of events that need to occur:

Monday	Tuesday	Wednesday	Thursday	Friday
Conduct Internet research on recycling.	Conduct Internet research on recycling.	Conduct Internet research on recycling.	Create questions for your interview of an expert on recycling.	Interview an expert on recycling.
Conduct any additional research that might be necessary.	Synthesize all the information you have gathered on the project.	Begin writing the summary of your findings.	Write the summary of your findings.	Complete the summary of your findings.

Because this is a guideline, students can decide when they need to do what. It may only take 2 days to conduct their research or it might take them 5. They will need to adjust to their needs. They may find they cannot procure an interview in the first week, pushing everything else back, and the paper will need to be written in a single day rather than the 3 allotted. Being able to manage your time is a skill that not many adults have the ability to do effectively. That is why teaching it to your students will be a valuable lifelong skill. Their ability to adapt to the management of their time will go a long way in making them valued 21st century workers.

EFFECTIVE ORAL AND WRITTEN COMMUNICATION

Public speaking is a valuable skill for any person to possess. One of the major reasons is that not everyone is able to do it. If you are someone who can do it and do it well, that is an advantage over others. How one gets good at public speaking is through experience. The more opportunities you give your students to speak publically without fear, the more comfortable they will become. Every experience you give them will provide that much more confidence in their ability. You build up this confidence over time until students are not only comfortable with public speaking, but until they are magnificent at it.

There are several reasons why the ability to publically speak is so important, but here are a few benefits for small business owners according to IMpro Solutions:

- Increased exposure
- Lead generation
- Establish credibility and trust
- Target a specific audience
- Gain a competitive edge
- Improve your reputation
- Share your knowledge
- Enhance your visibility
- Present yourself as an expert (Benefits of public speaking, n.d.)

Students get the same benefits from learning to publically speak.

One way to provide opportunities for students to publically speak is to have products in your PBL that involve oral presentation. Often times in the real world, people will have to give a presentation to their boss, colleagues, or a client. Modeling this act in your own projects will help students to get ready for that as well as giving them valuable experience in public speaking. And learning what goes into a successful or effective public presentation is also important to teach. From the position of body language, the tone of your voice, the use of visual aids, the persuasiveness of the speaker, the confidence they exude, all are things that students can work on, and get better at that will make them great public speakers.

This experience and confidence also applies to written communication. Have as many products as possible that involve written expression. This could be a research paper, debriefing, a business plan, journal entry, analysis, etc. The more students write across the curriculum, the stronger writers they will become.

CRITICAL THINKING AND PROBLEM SOLVING

The ability to problem solve is a skill students will use the rest of their lives. Think about how valuable an employee with strong problem-solving skills would be to an employer. Solving problems creatively and effectively saves money and leads to new clients. Although it seems at times like those with the ability to problem solve just have an innate ability to do so, somewhere in their experiences they learned this skill.

PBL is a way to problem solve. Students are given a job to do, and they must figure out how they are going to accomplish that task. How much creativity and how much innovation used in the project is the choice of the students, but they must come up with a solution to this problem. PBL allows for a lot of different problem-solving scenarios in a lot of different subject areas. It will provide students with a valuable lifelong skill that will benefit them in many ways.

Critical thinking is being able to think at a higher level. Most teachers are familiar with Bloom's Taxonomy. According to Bloom's there are six levels of thinking:

Remembering

Understanding

Applying

Analyzing

Evaluating

Creating

The first three, *remembering, understanding,* and *applying,* are considered lower-level thinking skills. Can a student recall information he or she has been told? Can students understand a concept or what a passage is telling them? Can they apply what they have learned to a different situation? We want all students to be able to function at these levels. The challenge to teachers is to tap into those higher levels of thinking. Can students analyze a reading and infer certain information that is not implicitly there? Can they evaluate a performance and give a clear explanation for what they used as their criteria and how they arrived at their opinion? Can they create something new taking the parts and skills of other work? Using PBL can have students *creating, evaluating,* and *analyzing* much easier than an objective multiple-choice test.

An example would be a research paper that is going to require students to critically think in order to complete the outline. This gets them thinking at the higher levels we want students to be tapping into. Besides the obviousness of thinking at a higher level, the advantage of being able to think critically is that you have multiple ideas for the same problem. Again, how valued would an employee who has the ability to think critically be to a business?

COLLABORATION ACROSS NETWORKS

No matter what situation you are in, you are going to be working with others the rest of your life. Especially if you find yourself in any sort of business, there is collaboration with your boss, team members, or clients. Being able to work with others is a skill that will make these relationships all the more easier. That is why collaboration is such a valuable skill for students to learn.

It is often a skill we do not teach in the classroom though. We might put students together for a group project, pair students up to work out a problem, or ask them to help one another, but how much purposeful, guided collaboration takes place in the classroom? When you just throw students together, like most things that are thrown, some things stick but others do not. Collaboration needs to be taught to students.

One way to do this is to make sure everyone understands their role in the group and exactly what is expected of them. There can sometimes be confusion because a student is unsure of what he or she is supposed to be doing or is just waiting around for someone to tell him or her what to do. Instead when they create their student contract, they should lay out what each person is responsible for. This does a couple of things. It lets the students know what their task at hand is. There is no sitting around waiting to be told what to do because it has very clearly been defined for that student. The second thing this does is allows for accountability. If the project manager is aware of who is supposed to be responsible for what, then he or she will hold the proper person accountable when things do not turn out the way they are supposed to. This also negates the unfair feeling many students experience when working in groups, which is that a bad group member pulls their grade down even though they worked hard.

Often times, because PBL takes the form of group projects, being able to collaborate well is going to make for better outcomes. Because you are working with students on the ability to collaborate, one natural by-product is that you will be teaching students leadership skills. This is someone with the confidence to step forward, share ideas, make others feel as though he or she is listening to their ideas, and inspire others to accomplish great things. It is an invaluable skill to have for any 21st century student.

At Least Manage This

The Partnership for 21st Century Skills (n.d.) provides this visual (Figure 2.1) for those skills considered valuable for a 21st century learner:

It is important for students to have a good grasp of 21st century skills, not just because it will help them in their schooling, but because

Figure 2.1   Framework for 21st Century Learning

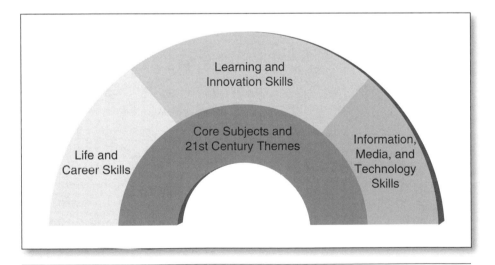

Partnership for 21st Century Learning. Reprinted with permission.

for any job they seek it will be a humongous advantage. Employers are seeking people who possess the following attributes:

1. Ability to access and analyze information

2. Curiosity and imagination

3. Initiative and entrepreneurialism

4. Adaptability

5. Effective oral and written communication

6. Critical thinking and problem solving

7. Ability to collaborate across networks

That is why it is important to set up your classroom as a 21st century classroom where these skills can be learned and honed. The best way to ensure your classroom is a 21st century one is by using PBL and managing your students. Having these skills not only covers the core subjects and 21st century survival skills, but it also will teach students life and career skills that will benefit them in the real world.

Setting Up Your Projects

Planning without action is futile, action without planning is fatal.

—Cornelius Fitchner

Thus far, this book has discussed the benefits of managing your classroom and the 21st century skills that can be taught using project-based learning (PBL). Now we are getting into the meat of the topic: How are you, the teacher, supposed to plan your lessons around PBL? Just like a project manager, you will need to provide your students with a task that they can work toward. You also will need to support your students in the creation of a solution to this task. Introduced in the book *Fundamentals of Project Management* (2007), the steps presented in Figure 3.1 are essentially the same steps you should follow when setting up and executing PBL in your classroom.

DEFINE THE PROBLEM

In the business world, the problem might be related to landing a lucrative client or providing support to a customer, or developing a new product that will make the company money. In the classroom, the problem is quite

Figure 3.1 Steps in Managing a Project

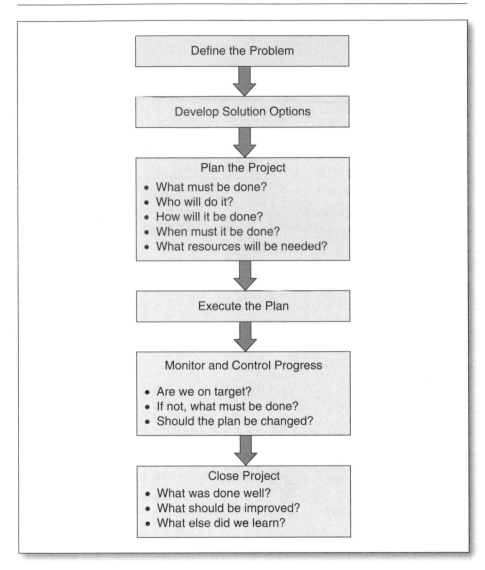

simple: What the heck do I teach my students? Luckily for you, most times the state has already defined the problem for you in the form of Common Core State Standards (CCSS). Here are some examples of CCSS in various subject areas:

Math Grade 8—Geometry

- Apply the Pythagorean Theorem to determine unknown side lengths in right triangles in real world and mathematical problems in two and three dimensions.

ELA—Grade 5

Craft and Structure: Literacy RL.5.4

- Determine the meaning of words and phrases as they are used in a text, including figurative language such as metaphors and similes.

And the Next Generation Standards various states are developing for Social Studies and Science:

Science Grade 6—California Department of Education

- Develop a model to describe the cycling of water through Earth's systems driven by energy from the sun and the force of gravity.

Social Studies Grade 4—New York Department of Education

- Students will map the voyages of Verrazano, Hudson, and Champlain and will determine which Native American peoples encountered these explorers.

The CCSS are being used in 43 states. These are the same for mathematics and English language arts in all of these states. Individual states have then chosen to develop state standards for science and social studies that might vary.

Even if your state is not using CCSS, your state more than likely has created standards of learning that teachers need to make sure students are learning in a given subject in a given year. These standards help to define the problem of what to teach the students. Many districts will create a map for teachers that can be used to guide what to teach as well. You can still use PBL in the classroom and follow the curriculum map. How to set up a project using CCSS as your problem will be discussed further in the next chapter.

DEVELOP SOLUTION OPTIONS

Even if you are using the CCSS to determine what you are teaching, the much more important question becomes just how you are going to teach it. The simple answer is through PBL. After all, you are reading this book to figure out how to do that very thing. But like most things in life, it is not that simple. There are many different ways to teach PBL with choices in how you deliver content, what activities students will be participating in, and what the product will look like. To make this easier, you should start with the end in mind, or in other words, the product. This is what marketers must do all the time. They have to be able to project themselves on both sides of the counter at the same time. Then they have to figure out how to take this product and explain it to the right person in the right way. As the teacher, you must do the same thing, determining what the end product will look like that shows students have mastered what it is they are supposed to be learning. Many times, a teacher wants to think of the most creative project he or she can. Your goal should not be to have students produce a flashy and entertaining product. The product needs to have some meat to it, it must deliver content. You have to balance the product between one that delivers content but also allows students to use their creativity.

An example of this would be having students produce a PowerPoint presentation lesson on conserving energy. The goal is for students to teach the rest of the class about methods of conserving energy using the format of a PowerPoint presentation. In addition to the value of the content is the value of the product because creating a visual presentation is something students might find themselves required to do when they are adults in the business world. The teacher can be as specific or as general as he or she wants to be in the format of the presentation. The more prescribed the format, the more likely that students will have a focused presentation. The less prescribed, the more creative students will be able to be although you do not want them to be creative at the cost of content. Teachers should get a feel for how much guidance a class will need. If you are working with a group that often gets off task and has trouble maintaining their focus, a prescribed format would be appropriate. If you have a responsible class that has proven it can handle time management and PBL, you might have much looser guidelines.

Let us say for the sake of argument you have decided on a format where students need to have at least 15 slides for their presentation, each slide must have a visual and limited text, the lesson should be in the 10- to 15-minute range, and every student in the group must talk in the presentation. As you visualize this product, just like marketers have to do, look at both sides of the counter, the teacher perspective and the student one. You need to ask yourself:

- Would this product allow students to show what they have learned about various methods of conserving energy?
- Does this product allow students to engage in higher levels of thinking and gain a deeper understanding of the topic than if they were just reading about it?
- Could such a product be assessed effectively by the teacher?

- Does the format chosen for the product allow students enough room for creativity but at the same time give them a platform to share what they have learned?
- Would this format of this product of having the various groups present to the class act as a blanket that covers many different aspects, or will they become tedious because they all are saying the same thing?

You have to make sure the product is a good fit for the topic. In this case, there are enough different ways to conserve energy that in hearing five groups present information on this, you are going to hear lots of different ways to do this. If students were teaching about the rock cycle, the content will be the same for everyone so having five groups present a PowerPoint on the exact same information might not be the best product for such a topic. A better product might be students creating a poster that can be turned in at the same time and assessed for the correct content. A good way to determine whether the product is a good fit or not is by visualizing yourself as an audience member. If you were someone who walked in from the street would this product demonstrate to you that the students who produced it learned something?

You should mix and match your products so that students are not doing the same thing all year long. You do not want students to do a PowerPoint as their product every single project. That would get tedious for you and them. Also after a couple of times they would have learned the skill of constructing a PowerPoint and should try to learn another skill. You could create your own list of products at the beginning of the year that would be possibilities to use as products. A list might look something like this:

- Video conference
- Prezi
- TED Talk
- Interview

- PowerPoint
- Debate
- Mock Trial
- Sales pitch

Chapter 7 will go into more detail what these products look like, but having a list such as this to plug into a project where it fits well is one way to approach it. To help generate this list of products, you might want to contact local area businesses and see what sorts of skills they are looking for in valuable employees. This might give you additional product choices as well as giving students a skill you know employers are looking for.

PLAN THE PROJECT

Once you have chosen the product and what that is going to look like, you have to figure out what steps must be followed in order to be able to create this product. Questions a teacher needs to ask himself or herself are the following:

- What must be done?
- Who will do it?
- How will it be done?
- When must it be done?
- What resources will be needed?

For instance, let us use our example of the PowerPoint. Starting from the end product, work backwards the skills and information students will need in order to successfully complete the project. When you are working backwards, you go back to the very next step students would need to accomplish in order to arrive at the one before it. In other words, you cannot jump from the presentation of the PowerPoint back to finding research. There are several steps in between that are being passed over. Instead, it might look something like this:

Figure 3.2 PowerPoint Project

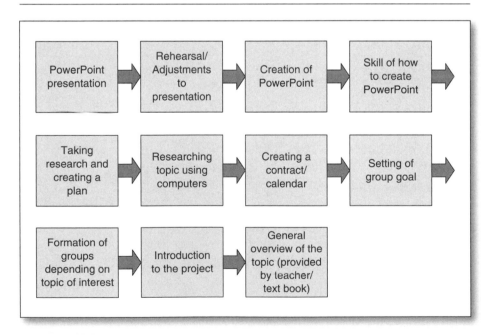

By breaking the project down as shown in Figure 3.2, you have given yourself clear steps on how to proceed with the project. In essence, it is planned. Now the teacher must determine how much time will be allotted to each of these skills (Figure 3.3).

Figure 3.3   Allotment of Time

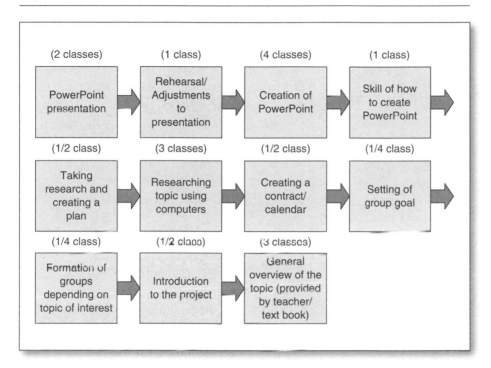

The way this has been planned out, it will take 16 classes to complete this project. One thing that would be helpful in your planning is to give a couple of days of padding to make sure students have enough time. You might have allotted three classes for research but come to find you need five. Or the creation of the contract might take longer than expected. The plan should be flexible to allow for adjustments should the progress of the students dictate this. When you are doing a project for the first time, you might plan for a certain amount of time and find what students really need is something very different. Adjust accordingly.

EXECUTE THE PLAN

There are two major steps to executing the plan. Step 1 is with the plan in place, you must take each of those steps and figure out how you are going to execute them individually. Do you know how to create a PowerPoint yourself so that you can show your students? Have you reserved the school computer lab for students to conduct their research? Have you made copies of the contracts and created a rubric that students can use to guide them? The project manager must figure out what resources are going to be needed and exactly what his or her role is in each step of the plan. Using our above example, teacher involvement during the general overview of the topic might be heavy due to delivering the content, but the research aspect might call for a very hands off approach with periodic check-ins to make sure students are where they need to be. The teacher needs to determine what his or her role for each of those steps is going to be and then execute that role just as a project manager would.

The second step in the execution of the plan is making sure the plan is clear to students. They are the workers who will be creating this product so it is of paramount importance that they understand just how they are to do this and what the expectations are. When you are introducing the project to students, in keeping with the project management aspect, give it to them like a job. It can even been issued in a memo much like a project manager would provide for his or her team. It might look something like this:

INTEROFFICE MEMORANDUM

SUBJECT

Coming to America

DATE: 8/25

PURPOSE

We will be going back to the year 1720. You have been challenged to create a campaign that will lure prospective residents into moving to your state. The 13 original colonies were formed on the eastern coast of the United States between the periods of 1607 through 1733 and included Massachusetts, Pennsylvania, North Carolina, South Carolina, Virginia, New York, New Jersey, New Hampshire, Rhode Island, Connecticut, Delaware, Georgia, and Maryland.

SUMMARY

You must incorporate the five themes of geography into the campaign, explaining each of them in relation to the state you are creating a campaign for:

1. Location

2. Place

3. Human and environment interaction

4. Movement

5. Regions

QUESTIONS TO CONSIDER

- Why did people settle where they did?
- What did each of the colonies have to offer both good and bad to those settling there?
- How did they determine where one colony started and another began?

RECOMMENDATION

Product: You will create two visual aids to convince people to come to your state.

1. *Poster* should focus on the five themes of geography and what the state has to offer in regard to them.

2. *Brochure* should be a persuasive pamphlet giving people the reasons why they should settle in your state. There should be maps and visuals included to back up your claims.

CRITERIA FOR EVALUATION

Your product will be evaluated using three criteria:

1. Content: Do you back up your statements with researched evidence?

2. Visual aids: Do your poster and brochure look professional?

3. Maps: Do you include at least five maps to illustrate the lure of your state?

You would present this to the class as a job and lay out the timeline that you determined when creating your plan (there are templates for creating your own memo in the Reproducibles section). You can even provide students with calendars that chart their progress with deadlines. Show them examples of the product you are asking them to create. If you want them to create a podcast, give them exemplary examples of podcasts, if you are having a TED Talk as the product, show them a couple to demonstrate what they are like and what successful ones look like, if you are asking them to create an artifact in a museum, show them displays of museums such as the Smithsonian or British Museum to give them an idea of how a professional would do it. If possible, show past student products, both good and not so good, to demonstrate what you are looking for. Collecting products at the end of a project is always valuable to next year's students and beyond. If it is the first time you have done this product you might have to produce one yourself to give them an idea of the expectations.

The second way to make sure students are clear with the project is to provide them with a rubric for how they will be evaluated. This sets out a clear criteria for how their end product will be assessed. It also forces you the teacher to have a clear vision for what you are looking for. If you are unsure of what you want students to produce, how will they have a clear idea of how to proceed? When you give them a rubric it acts as a blueprint for how to create a successful product. A rubric for the Coming to America project might look like this:

Coming to America

Students: _____ State: _____

Overall	Content	Visual Aids	Maps
Excellent (A)	• Includes many details and examples designed to back up each of the five themes of geography. • Research is accurate and gives a clear picture of the theme it is supposed to be demonstrating. • Research is taken from the perspective of someone from the 1700s.	• Visual aids look professional, like something that would be found in a visitor's bureau. • Poster clearly conveys the five themes of geography in regard to your state. • The brochure is very persuasive in its argument for why one should settle in this state.	• Between the brochure and the poster includes at least five different maps that show the various reasons people would want to settle there. • Maps can easily be seen. • It is clear what the maps are showing.

Overall	Content	Visual Aids	Maps
Good (B–C)	• Has a few details and examples to back up five themes but could use more. • Research is accurate but does not give a clear picture of the theme, showing one aspect rather than a well-rounded picture. • Most of the time the research is taken from the perspective of someone from the 1700s but a couple of instances where there are references to modern times.	• One visual aid looks professional, like something that would be found in a visitor's bureau, but the other one has elements that make it look non-professional. • Poster conveys the five themes of geography in regard to your state but what it is conveying is not consistently clear. • The brochure is persuasive in its argument for why one should settle in this state in parts but could use more evidence to make the argument.	• Between the brochure and the poster includes at least four different maps that show the various reasons people would want to settle there. • Most of the maps can easily be seen but one or two are hard to make out. • It is not always clear what the maps are showing either because it is not explained or labeled.
Needs Improvement (D–F)	• Does not use details and examples to back up the five themes. • Research is inaccurate, giving the audience the wrong idea about the themes or a very limited view. • Many instances where the poster/pamphlet refers to the modern state rather than when it was first forming.	• Visual aids do not look professional, but like something put together without much thought to how nice it looks. • Poster does not clearly convey the five themes of geography in regard to your state, causing some confusion in what it is trying to convey. • The brochure is not very persuasive in its argument for why one should settle in this state, lacking any examples or evidence of attractive geographic features in the state.	• Between the brochure and the poster includes three or less maps that show the various reasons people would want to settle there. • Many of the maps cannot easily be seen either because they are too small or blurry. • It is not clear what the maps are showing; it seems like they were just thrown on there without understanding what it was trying to convey.

Notice the rubric uses the same criteria in the headings as were contained in the memo. It also shows students what an excellent, good, and not so good physically looks like, allowing them to gain a greater sense for what their own product should look like. Chapter 8 will go into much more detail on how to use and create rubrics, but it is important to provide or create this at the very beginning of the project so that students are clear on what they are to be doing and how they will be evaluated. Waiting until the end does not make these aspects clear to students, and you will get unfocused products.

MONITOR AND CONTROL PROGRESS

You have introduced the project and made it clear to students what the expectations are with a memo and a rubric. Now you just sit back and watch them work, right? Not quite. As a project manager you must monitor and control student progress. This can be done in a heavy-handed or more laid back approach. A good project manager is somewhere in the middle of this spectrum. The project manager is making himself accessible so that workers can come to him when there are issues with the project or just to help them get unstuck. At the same time, he is not micromanaging the workers, making them feel like they are being so closely monitored that they are unable to make any mistakes or that they are not trusted.

One of the most challenging aspects to balance in a PBL classroom is getting enough assessments. If students are working on a 4-week project, does that mean the only grade that will occur in that 4 weeks will be the final product? A project manager does not wait for 4 weeks before giving feedback and evaluating progress. In a PBL classroom, the teacher should figure out a way to assess the process as much as the product. There are a few strategies for doing this. The first is monitoring progress through observation. The role of the teacher in this case is to observe the process students are going through. Are they learning new skills, have they synthesized the information needed adequately, are they using higher-level thinking to accomplish their task? These are all valuable skills that might not show in the final product, but are important to the education of a student nonetheless. Having a way to assess this process is important when working on PBL.

How you the teacher can monitor this process is by using a project management tool known as the One-Page Project Manager, which was adapted from the book *The One-Page Project Manager: Communicate and Manage Any Project With a Single Sheet of Paper* by Clark Campbell (2006). It allows the teacher to monitor progress through observation and to record the progress of students. A One-Page Project Manager looks like this (blank forms can be found in the Reproducibles section):

Goals			Major Tasks	Project Deadline														Responsible Party				
Goal # 1	Goal # 2	Goal # 3		Day 1	Day 2	Day 3	Day 4	Day 5	Day 6	Day 7	Day 8	Day 9	Day 10	Day 11	Day 12	Day 13	Day 14	Group member # 1	Group member # 2	Group member # 3	Group member # 4	Group member # 5

The teacher would have the group fill this out at the beginning of the project. This could be used as the student contract. Students would place their goals in the goal columns, list out all the tasks that must be accomplished in order to complete the product, and indicate who is responsible for which tasks. A completed One-Page Project Manager for the Coming to America project would look like this:

Project Deadline: January 25

Goals	Major Tasks	Day 1	Day 2	Day 3	Day 4	Day 5	Day 6	Day 7	Day 8	Day 9	Day 10	Day 11	Day 12	Day 13	Day 14	Group member # 1: Chad	Group member # 2: Bonnie	Group member # 3: Tracy	Group member # 4: Ben	Group member # 5
	Complete contract/Set goals	X														X	X	X	X	
	Research colony of New Jersey		X	X	X											X	X	X	X	
	Synthesize the research into bullet points					X													X	
	Create a rough draft of the brochure						X	X								X	X			
	Find maps/photos for use in the poster						X	X										X	X	
	Design a final draft on the computer of brochure								X	X	X	X	X			X	X			
	Get the posterboard								X									X		
	Print up photos/maps for use on poster									X									X	
	Create poster										X	X	X					X	X	
	Make sure poster from perspective of 1700s													X				X	X	
	Make sure brochure from perspective of 1700s													X		X	X			
	Use rubric to go over brochure														X	X		X	X	
	Use rubric to go over poster														X	X	X	X		

Goals

Goal # 1: Complete the project on time

Goal # 2: Get an A on the project

Goal # 3: Work together well

This group has decided to split the responsibilities among the group, making Chad and Bonnie responsible for the brochure, and Tracy and Ben in charge of the poster. This gives group members clear tasks they need to accomplish. They have also plotted out when each activity should take place, giving them an idea of progress. The teacher can then use this sheet to record and monitor the progress of the students through observation. Are the responsible people working on what they are supposed to be? Are students meeting the due dates of the various parts of the project? When they are finishing up a particular task, what is the quality of it? The One-Page Project Manager sheet allows the teacher to keep a record of the process the students are using, giving her another way to assess students besides just the final product.

Another way to assess student progress is through the use of progress-monitoring meetings. These are scheduled and unscheduled meetings run by the teacher/project manager to determine the progress of the group. The teacher sits down with the group to have a conversation about how the group is doing. She might look at student notes, at drafts of the product, or ask questions to check for understanding. Some other questions the teacher might ask are

- Are we on target?
- If not what must be done?
- Should the plan be changed?

Using the Coming to America project, students will be working on it for 14 days. Scheduling a meeting every 3 or 4 days would allow the teacher to check in with the group to determine their progress. The teacher could use this meeting to assess the quality of the student effort and the task they are performing. The teacher could choose to have these meetings with individual members of the group or as a whole. There could also be nonscheduled meetings when the teacher observes a group struggling or just wants to hear about the progress and thus calls for a meeting. This meeting can be used to get the group back on track or to share successes. The types of meetings a project manager/teacher can hold will be discussed further in Chapter 5.

A third way to monitor and control progress is through self/peer monitoring. This will be discussed in more detail in Chapter 8, but it involves having students evaluate one another throughout the process of the project. There would be periodic times when students would give themselves and each group member a grade based on their effort so far. In the example of the geography project, students might do a self/peer evaluation after the research aspect, another during the creation of the rough draft, and then the efforts toward the final draft. Self/peer review is good because instead of having one set of teacher eyes, you now have all the eyes in the classroom, and these eyes see everything. There might be a student who is very adept at looking busy whenever the teacher is walking by but then does very little other times. The group would be aware of this and reflect this in their self/peer evaluations. The teacher would then collect these self/peer evaluations and use them as part of the assessment of the project.

Whichever method the teacher chooses, there should be an assessment of the process as well as the product. Many times the best instances of learning take place during the process, and it is important to assess students properly on this.

CLOSE PROJECT

Usually the final aspect to a unit of learning is the summative assessment. Students take the test and then move on to the next topic that needs to be learned. In the project management classroom, there is an additional step to the project, and that is the reflection. The reflection closes the project. Questions to consider for this would be

- What was done well?
- What should be improved?
- What else did we learn?

It is best to find a reflection protocol to use with students that enables them to really analyze what they learned. This reflection should not be graded or used to assess their performance. It needs to be a vehicle where students can share their feelings honestly and determine the lesson they took from the project, not what the teacher wanted them to. Here are some methods of reflection that can be used as suggested by Arthur L. Costa and Bena Kalick (2009) in their book *Learning and Leading With Habits:*

Discussion: This is a teacher-led forum where through discussion, students share their feelings toward the project both looking at the process and the product. They might reflect upon their own habits, mistakes that were made, successes that they found, and other such insights of learning. Although the teacher is guiding the discussion, he or she should be doing more listening than talking. The role of the teacher here is as the facilitator of the discussion, asking follow up questions to achieve deeper levels of thinking and helping students to gain an understanding of just what it is they learned, good or bad.

Interviews: These can be done one-on-one or with the group. In the interview, the teacher should ask the students how they think the project went and why they felt it was either a success or had room for improvement. This provides a more intimate setting, and students might be willing to open up more if there is a smaller group or just themselves. The teacher can even have students interview one another to determine what was learned or the group can interview itself if the project used groups.

Questioning: Questioning can be in the form of verbal responses or written ones. Unlike a discussion that has a lot of back and forth, the questioning has the teachers providing prompts for what to think about. Students can share their insights, feelings, understandings, and how to apply what they have learned.

Logs and Journals: The advantage to logs and journals is that it provides a written record of the student's thoughts that can be looked at later to provide further reflection. A student can look at their progression over a series of projects to determine their growth.

No matter which method you choose, having a purposeful reflection at the end of the project is an effective way to close a project and bring learning to its fullest.

At Least Manage This

The basic steps in any project are the following:

1. Define the problem

2. Develop solution options

3. Plan the project

4. Execute the plan

5. Monitor and control progress

6. Close project (Lewis, 2006, p. 15)

The planning phase involves the first three steps. This is where a bulk of the work is going to be done by the teacher, but if you develop a sound project, the execution of the plan becomes that much easier. The execution, monitoring, and closing of the project can all be generated by the students, which makes sense because they are the ones supposed to be learning, and thus they are the ones supposed to be doing a majority of the work. If you set up your projects correctly, the students should be working harder than the teacher, which is the way it should be.

Linking the Projects
to the Standards

Creating a Mission Statement

> *A mission statement is not something you write overnight . . . But fundamentally, your mission statement becomes your constitution, the solid expression of your vision and values. It becomes the criterion by which you measure everything else in your life.*
>
> —Stephen Covey

Almost every business worth its salt has a mission statement that acts as the backbone of the company. Some examples of these would be Microsoft, whose mission statement is to enable people and businesses throughout the world to realize their full potential. Or Google who strives to organize the world's information and make it universally accessible and useful. School districts also have mission statements, usually pertaining to the education and growth of students as well as providing an excellent atmosphere to foster student interests, abilities, and needs. Why have a mission statement? According to Small Business by Demand Media, "the benefit of creating a mission statement is that it establishes a business's underlying purpose beyond the simple goal . . . this purpose can help guide the types of products and services the company offers as well as the company's policies" (Hamel, n.d.).

What is the mission statement of your classroom? It is probably somewhere along the lines of the school mission statement, the successful teaching of students, but having such a general mission statement does not provide the focus needed for projects. You need to create a mission statement for each project your class undertakes, and it will be this that drives the project forward and informs your decisions as a teacher. The good news for you is that the mission statements for your classroom have already been developed. These come in the form of the content standards that most states are using at this point. You just need to figure out how to connect the project to the mission statement so that the end product is a reflection of this content standard.

STARTING WITH THE CONTENT STANDARD

When you first sit down to plan out your project as outlined in Chapter 3, you have to consider what is it that students need to get from this project, what is the takeaway they will be held accountable for? By using the Common Core State Standards (CCSS), you are providing students with the building blocks they need in order to be successful on these high-stakes tests, while at the same time, teaching them 21st century skills that will enable them to be successful in the real world. Depending on the length of your project, you can link a single content standard. For example, take this CCSS from language arts Grade 2 writing:

> Write opinion pieces in which they introduce the topic or book they are writing about, state an opinion, supply reasons that support the opinion, use linking words (e.g., because, and, also) to connect opinion and reasons, and provide concluding statement or section.

Knowing this is the mission statement and should be what drives the project, you need to consider what sort of product students would need to produce to show mastery of such a content standard. The verbs provide clues as to what this product needs to look like: "*Write* opinion pieces" indicates the product needs to be a written format. Additionally the word *pieces* means there needs to be more than one. In those writing pieces, students must state an opinion and then support it. Your project needs to be set up to allow students to do this.

Given that the standard is asking for pieces, you will want to consider two or more texts for students to provide their opinion on. To keep it simple, you could pick two fairy tales: *Hansel and Gretel*, and *Jack and the Beanstalk*. A final product might be a newspaper review where the student must give their opinion on which story she enjoyed more and why this was, citing textual examples to back her opinion. You would have to provide some direction to ensure students use linking words, maybe by providing an exemplary example or doing one together as a class.

That would be the product at its simplest level. There are several additional things to consider however. Are there other CCSS this particular project could measure? Under the reading CCSS is the following:

Recount stories, including fables and folktales from diverse cultures, and determine their central message, lesson, or moral.

This content standard could be addressed in multiple forms whether it be in the finished product, content quizzes, checking for understanding in discussion, or other assessments designed to determine the central message, lesson, or moral.

There is nothing in the selected CCSS about having to read the text so as the teacher you could go a few different directions. You could have the students read the fairy tales themselves, you could read the stories aloud to the students, or you could have them watch a cartoon that illustrates the stories. If you chose the latter, under the listening CCSS is one that states:

Recount or describe key ideas or details from a text read aloud or information presented orally or through other media.

This would cover the teacher reading the text aloud or showing a cartoon of the stories. Again you would need to have some assessment that measures that students can indeed recount or describe key details. This could come in the final product or it could come in other forms of assessment.

You also have choices in what stories you use with students. You could choose to tell the same story, just from another perspective. For instance, there is the story *Alaska's Three Pigs* by Arlene Laverde and Mindy Dwyer that takes the story and places it in the frigid environment of Alaska. Students could look at things such as perspective or setting, while still providing their opinion on the stories as with the original content standard. By doing this you could add another CCSS in reading:

Compare and contrast two or more versions of the same story (e.g., Cinderella stories) by different authors or from different cultures.

Or this one:

Compare and contrast the most important points presented by two texts on the same topic.

As you can see, one small project with a single content standard can grow to cover several different content standards. You just have to be purposeful how you measure those standards to ensure mastery. You could not have one single product where you give a single grade that shows the mastery. You would either have to come up with other ways to assess the standards, or you would have to be specific in the rubric of the product what standard is being measured when. A rubric for the end product might look something like this:

FAIRY TALE REVIEW

Student: _____

	Review W-1	Content RL-2	Comparison RL-9
Excellent A	• Student shares in detail his or her opinion of which story was preferred, supplying clear reasons that support the opinion. • Review uses linking words such as because, and, and also throughout the piece. • Review provides a concluding statement that summarizes in detail the opinion of the reviewer and the reasons for it.	• Using details and examples from the text the student is able to recount the basic story of both tales. • Student is able to determine with clarity the central lesson or moral of the story.	• Student compares the similarities between the two stories using many examples to make the comparison. • Student points out the differences in the two stories providing plenty of examples, identifying why the same story is different.
Good (B–C)	• Student shares in his or her opinion of which story was preferred, supplying reasons that support the opinion, but opinion is not always detailed and/or support not always clear. • Review uses linking words such as because, and, and also in the piece but not consistently. • Review provides a concluding statement that summarizes the opinion of the reviewer and the reasons for it but lacks detail needed for clarity.	• Student is able to recount the basic story of both tales but does not provide enough detail and/or examples to paint a clear picture. • Student is able to determine the central lesson or moral of the story but is not able to express it in depth, just at a surface level.	• Student compares the similarities between the two stories but does not provide many examples from the text in doing so. • Student points out the differences in the two stories but does not provide enough examples to identify why the same story is different.

	Review W-1	**Content RL-2**	**Comparison RL-9**
Needs Work (D–F)	• Student does not share his or her opinion of which story was preferred, either neglecting reasons that support the opinion or simply not stating it. • Review does not use linking words such as *because, and,* and *also* in the piece. • Review either does not provide a concluding statement that summarizes the opinion of the reviewer or it lacks details needed for clarity.	• Student is not able to recount the basic story of both tales or lacks any detail and/or examples. • Student is not able to determine the central lesson or moral of the story, either neglecting it or misunderstanding it.	• Student does not compare the similarities between the two stories. • Student does not point out the differences in the two stories.

There are three content standards being addressed with this rubric, and they are all evaluating very different standards. A student could score an excellent in the review aspect of the piece but then fail to conduct a comparison of the pieces, resulting in not having mastered that particular content standard. It shows the teacher and student which standards the student is successful with and those that might need more work. How to create such a rubric will be addressed in Chapter 8.

WORKING BACKWARDS

One strategy that can be used when planning a project to ensure it is well implemented is the method of backwards building. What that means is a teacher starts the project by envisioning what the ideal final product would look like. Backwards building uses the model established by Wiggins and McTighe (2005) and looks like this:

1. First, identify what will be accomplished.

2. Determine what product will best show what you have learned.

3. Plan how you will develop and execute this product.

If the backwards building process is followed when creating the lesson, effective projects that accurately assess whether a student attains mastery are possible. Here is an example of a math CCSS from the third grade:

Explain equivalence of fractions in special cases, and compare fractions by reasoning about their size.

a. Understand two fractions as equivalent (equal) if they are the same size, or the same point on a number line.

b. Recognize and generate simple equivalent fractions, e.g., 1/2 = 2/4, 4/6 = 2/3. Explain why the fractions are equivalent, e.g., by using a visual fraction model.

c. Express whole numbers as fractions, and recognize fractions that are equivalent to whole numbers. *Examples: Express 3 in the form 3 = 3/1; recognize that 6/1 = 6; locate 4/4 and 1 at the same point of a number line diagram.*

Using these CCSS answers the question of the mission statement. Students will master the math skills regarding fractions. Next is envisioning a final product. A teacher could have students create a recipe book. Each student is responsible for submitting a recipe that must contain several fractions where the student analyzes the CCSS to display a mastery of that skill. This is the development of solution options. The recipe book is the end product but students must master an understanding of the fractions in order to write and analyze their recipe. The assessment would break down into three parts, the three parts of the CCSS that need to be demonstrated. The final product might look something like this:

Recipe for Chocolate Chip Cookies

Ingredients

- 2 1/4 cups all-purpose flour
- 1 teaspoon baking soda
- 1 teaspoon salt
- 1 teaspoon vanilla extract
- 1 cup (2 sticks) butter, softened
- 3/4 cup granulated sugar
- 3/4 cup packed brown sugar
- 2 large eggs
- 1/2 cup chocolate chips or 2 1/4 cups of chocolate chips

1 tablespoon of product

Here would be the student analysis of each of the CCSS earmarked for this project:

a. Understand two fractions as equivalent (equal) if they are the same size, or the same point on a number line.

For example, even though the granulated sugar and the brown sugar are two different substances, the measurement of them is equivalent because the same size measuring spoon was used.

b. Recognize and generate simple equivalent fractions, e.g., $1/2 = 2/4$, $4/6 = 2/3$. Explain why the fractions are equivalent, e.g., by using a visual fraction model.

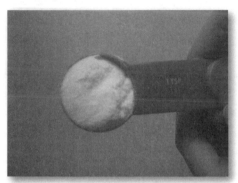

The 1/2 cup of chocolate chips remains the same whether you divide the cup into halves or fourths. In other words, 1/2 cup would be equivalent to two 1/4 cups.

   c. Express whole numbers as fractions, and recognize fractions that are equivalent to whole numbers. *Examples:* Express 3 in the form 3 = 3/1; recognize that 6/1 = 6; locate 4/4 and 1 at the same point of a number line diagram.

Is the same as

There are 3 teaspoons per tablespoon. That means my teaspoon of salt, vanilla, and baking soda are equivalent to 1 tablespoon of product or a 3/1.

Students have to demonstrate a mastery in their explanation of the recipe to show that they understand the CCSS. The use of examples from the recipe illustrates this understanding, and as an extra bonus, it has been applied to a real-world situation taking it to the domain D of the rigor/relevance chart.

With the CCSS determining what will be accomplished and the envisioning of the final product, now the teacher must figure out how to plan this project. Students will obviously need to learn certain skills before they can begin to analyze their recipe. As mentioned in the previous chapter, start at the end and work your way backwards with the idea of what would be the next logical step that would lead to the end (Figure 4.1):

Figure 4.1   Fractions in the Kitchen Project

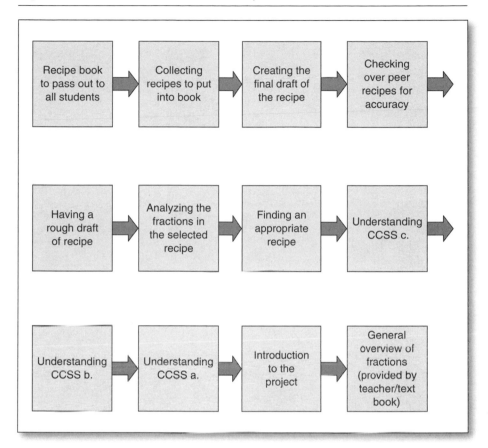

The teacher could allocate however many days he or she feels is necessary for each of the tasks and plan accordingly. The first time through a project, these estimations might not be correct, so make sure to give yourself a little wiggle room either way if a lesson goes faster than anticipated or it seems obvious from student reaction that they are not comprehending the lesson.

At Least Manage This

When planning a project, it is essential to link the heart of the project to a specific content standard that needs to be covered whether that be CCSS or a learning objective determined by the teacher. You have the choice to link many standards to a single project, but must be careful that you are measuring mastery for each of these content standards.

Otherwise, a student might not know what he or she still needs to master in regard to the content. One method of planning involves backwards building and starts with the final product in mind, building backwards the skills and activities required to reach this final product.

Collaboration in the 21st Century Classroom

No one can whistle a symphony. It takes a whole orchestra.

—H. E. Luccock

The four *Cs* are the skills educators have determined are important for a 21st century learner to possess. They are

1. Creativity and innovation

2. Critical thinking and problem solving

3. Communication

4. Collaboration

This book has already discussed the first three. The last one is of great importance to successfully running your classroom like a project manager. If a student is someone who is able to collaborate with others well, and others want to work with him or her, the student will go far in the business world. With the use of project-based learning (PBL) in your classroom, you will often have times when students will be working as part of a unit. And just like a project manager in the business world, you need to shape this unit so that it is able to accomplish great things, greater than if any one of the people had been working by himself. Otherwise, why would you have people complete tasks as part of a group?

Some of the benefits of collaboration in the workplace according to Bright Hub (Jones, 2010):

1. **The Collaborative Process Combines Different Perspectives**. When individuals from various professional and technical backgrounds come together to work on a project, the result is that all angles are considered. This is a particularly attractive outcome, especially in situations where the project is expected to command a huge budget, because it eliminates the possibility of errors arising out of failures and considers the effect of contributing elements.

2. **Workplace Collaboration Encourages Creativity**. Bringing together several different voices from within an organization helps to raise the profile of ideas that may never have come to the forefront if not for the collaborative effort. Teams that are well structured consist of staff members from various levels of the company, and these individuals naturally bring with them their outlook on the project. Creative solutions are often the result of simply looking at challenges from a different angle.

3. **Collaboration Takes Advantage of Synergies**. The formation of collaborative teams often involves the separation of duties. Within the structure of the team, certain members may be asked to focus on particular elements and put forth a recommendation based on their expertise. This kind of separation of responsibilities helps to bring the benefit of synergy to the project because areas of overlap are more easily identified, and the incidences of re-doing work can be eliminated.

4. **Workplace Collaboration Brings Balance to Decision Making**. The influence of several different stakeholders that may comprise the overall team helps to ensure that the decisions made are ones that consider the effect of all the interested parties. This means that workplace collaboration can root out the occurrence of biased or partisan decisions because each stakeholder has a presence around the table.

5. **Collaboration May Improve Delivery Times**. If the stakeholders are able to recognize their synergies and leverage the experience of all the parties represented, a project that is a collaborative effort has the potential to be completed on or even before schedule.

How do you use collaboration in the PBL 21st century classroom? Collaboration means more than just putting students together in a group and telling them to produce a product. Teamwork is something that can be taught. You as the project manager need to guide this collaboration and foster it.

SKILL OF COLLABORATION

If you have decided to make group work a large part of your PBL classroom, you should dedicate some time at the beginning of the school year when you are involved in the orientation and training of your students to teach a purposeful lesson on how to collaborate. Purposeful means that you do not just do a beginning of the year activity where you have students working in groups. It means the lesson itself is explicitly teaching students how to collaborate.

The first thing the group members should do is get to know one another. This does not mean finding out everyone's favorite color or what they want to do as a career, but getting to know their working styles and how they perform their best. One mistake groups often make is assuming everyone works the same. This causes problems because when one group member is doing a task differently than another member, it can cause rifts within the group. It is important for members of the group to recognize the differences members of the group have and then assign tasks accordingly. There are several activities that a teacher can facilitate in order for students to learn about each other. One of these is called Compass Points (activity can be found in the Reproducibles). The idea of Compass Points is that students identify with one of the four cardinal directions based on the type of person they are

North: Action, get it done

West: Details, organization, scheduler

East: Study, analyze, think about it

South: People person, everyone feels heard, make sure everyone is on board

Although students might have some qualities from multiple directions (the student might be a detailed person who likes to analyze), they must choose only one of the directions under the criteria that it is the one that best fits them. Once the students have chosen what direction best applies to them, then group the students in the room by their direction. Have all the norths stand at the top of the room, all the souths at the bottom, and so on. When they are in these groups, have them discuss the following questions:

- Use adjectives to describe strengths from your compass direction.
- Use adjectives to describe weaknesses from your compass direction.
- Which compass direction do you think you would work best with? Which would be the most challenging?
- If your team did not have a compass direction, how do you think it would function?

Give students a little bit of time to have their discussion and then have the group report out their findings. What should organically come from these discussions is that certain directions do not work well with other directions. The north with their get it done attitude do not want to wait for the east to study and analyze the situation. But the reason these groups do not work well together is not because of a personality issue, but because of a difference in the way they approach the work. The final question is designed to help people realize that as great as a bunch of norths would be at getting something done quickly, there would be details overlooked that would make the quality of the work suffer. And a group full of easts would certainly have some interesting, thought-provoking discussions, but they would not come to a conclusion in a timely manner. You need a mixture of the directions in order to make sure all bases are covered. The north acts as the rudder moving the group forward, the west ensures that everyone is getting done what they are supposed to, the east brings depth to the conversation and considers all options, and the south is the peacekeeper who makes sure everyone's voice is being heard.

Ideally all groups would have a north, south, east, and west, but we know that cannot always happen. However, recognizing that you have people in your group that might approach a project differently than you is important for group harmony and understanding the motivation of others. Group harmony is very different than everyone in the group liking one another. Group harmony is a group working effectively despite the fact that people might not get along for the benefit and advancement of the project.

Now that students are aware of the differences, the next step should be to do a group activity, mixing in people from different directions. One such icebreaker activity is the Mission to Mars scenario. The Mission to Mars icebreaker is relatively simple and can be altered to fit the needs of the teacher. It starts with the following scenario:

Earth has decided to inhabit the planet Mars. They have created an environment where a limited number of people can live. They are hoping whomever colonizes the planet will eventually grow into a civilization. You have 20 people who have applied for the trip but only 10 spots. You must decide who is included in the Mission to Mars?

Then on 20 index cards, you write 20 such persons. It might look something like this:

Teacher (male)	Taylor Swift (female)
Pregnant woman	Doctor (female)
7 year old (male)	Soldier with a gun (male)
Pastor (male)	Scientist with cancer (female)
Carpenter (female)	Historian (male)
Electrician (female)	Gay musician (male)
Politician (male)	Computer expert (female)
80 year old (female)	Lawyer (male)
Farmer (male)	Engineer who is in a wheelchair (female)
Lebron James (male)	Escaped prisoner (female)

As a group, students have an allotted amount of time to work together to whittle the list from 20 to 10, giving sound arguments for why they selected who they did as well as why they did not keep others. You might even assign specific roles to members of the group. Each group has:

Leader: Organizes the group and makes sure they stay on task

Scribe: Records the decisions of the group

Spokesperson: Speaks for the group when addressing the entire class

Timekeeper: Keeps track of time and how much is left for the activity

By having specific roles everyone knows what their contribution to the group needs to be and can be held accountable if they are not doing their part. Let students assign these roles based on their direction and their strengths. At the end of the time, have the group report out using their spokesperson. There can be follow up questions or class discussions as to who was picked and why.

An icebreaker activity such as this establishes the foundation for collaboration in the classroom. Once students figure out the format of groups and how they can successfully work together, the next step is to build the endurance for working in a group for a longer-term project. Students can put differences aside and work together if it is just for one class period, but if they have a 3-week project, can they collaborate successfully to produce a quality product.

SETTING NORMS

One way to establish this endurance for longer projects is the use of norms. Norms stands for normal, in other words, what would it look like if you walked into a normal classroom with students interacting with one another. Norms are very different than rules. Rules are usually determined by an authority figure who is then responsible for enforcing these rules. Norms are simply the expectations the group has set. An example of this would be picking your nose. There is no rule or law that says you should not pick your nose, but societal norms dictate that doing such an act is gross or against the normal way of behaving. And you are not judged by one person but by everyone who has accepted that act as disgusting. Group norms follow the same concept. They are not rules, but they are how everyone expects the group members to act when working together. If someone does not follow the group norms, rather than the teacher having to enforce her rules, the students point out how the member is breaking the norm and react as though this is not a normal way to behave in a group. Norms carry more weight and power with students if you allow them to create them. If these are simply rules handed down by the teacher, there is no ownership for students. The fact they help to write them makes the students remember the norms better; the norms are more instinctual to follow because of this familiarity.

What the creation of norms looks like is you give students five to seven sticky notes and provide them with the following prompt: What do you need in order to be successful in a group? Make sure to frame this in a positive aspect (in other words do not have students write what causes them to be unsuccessful). Have students draw on their past experiences working in groups and what allowed them to collaborate effectively. Students might need a little guidance in what a successful group looks like. A successful group in a school setting is one where the members of the group are able to accomplish their task and produce high-quality work. This does not mean members of the group all like one another. One thing students and teachers often get confused about is they believe members of a group need to get along. They want groups where everyone is nice to one another and get along perfectly. They might even create a norm of "be nice to one another." The reality is that not all people get along. For whatever reason whether it be past history, attitudes, or a perception, some members of the group are not going to get along with one another, but here is the thing: That is alright! The 1978 New York Yankees hated one another. Regardless of the fact that they did not get along, they still played together as a team. They trailed the Boston Red Sox by 14 games in July but managed to catch the Red Sox and force a one game playoff which they won. They went on to win the World Series. The question students and teachers need to think about is whether it is more important to have someone nice in your group that produces substandard work, or someone who is not as likeable but does a really good job? Businesses would want the second guy. Businesses are not in business so that people can all get along. Businesses are in business to be productive.

Have students write one need per sticky note. After giving them some time to do this, invite them up to the board or a piece of butcher paper hanging on the wall and have them cluster with other students similar norms. If eight people had something about being respectful, stick all of those sticky notes together. Or maybe half the class thought it was important to meet deadlines that then becomes a norm. What happens fairly quickly is that you see what is important to the class as a whole. If there is an outlier sticky note with no other similar stickies, then the issue is specific to that student and not necessarily the class as a whole and might not be a norm. From these clusters create anywhere from five to seven norms the class can agree to (many more than seven can cause things to become confusing). It might look something like this:

- Respect others thoughts, actions, and ideas.
- Everyone needs to contribute to their group by doing the task assigned.
- Be willing to share ideas and compromise.
- Stay on task and be willing to refocus when asked.
- Be responsible for the tasks you are assigned.
- Work should be of high quality.

Some norms might need adjusted to fit the needs of all students. For example, if it were suggested to use "get an A on projects" as a norm, and yet there were people who are unwilling or unable to meet that norm, then it should not be made a norm. Notice also how all the norms are put in a positive connotation. They very easily could have looked like this:

- Do not be disrespectful to others thoughts, actions, and ideas.
- If someone is not contributing they should be punished.
- Do not block other people's ideas.
- Do not get off task.
- Get done what you say you will get done.
- Work should not be of poor quality.

The norms are similar in spirit but in looking at both lists, you can see how the positive list will encourage positive collaboration.

Once the list has been formed and all students agree with it, the list should be written down or printed up and displayed in the classroom. You can even provide copies to students and have them keep it in their folder. This way, students are reminded of what the norms are, and it will help them in their group behavior. Students should be reminded these norms are not set in stone and can be changed if things do not seem to be working. Maybe an additional norm needs to be included to stop a certain behavior or one does not seem to be effective and thus is stricken from the list. The most important thing is to make sure the norms are revisited from time to time to ensure they are not forgotten about. Even just going over them again at the beginning of the project reminds students of the expectations they created.

DIVIDING UP TASKS

When students are working in groups, it is important to create specific assignments for students. Go back to the example of the 1978 New York Yankees: although they hated one another, they were able to still work together to win games because each person was very clear on what his role with the team was and as long as he did what was expected of him, the team was going to succeed.

If no specific roles are assigned, everyone in the group will work on everything, which can cause confusion for group members in exactly what their role is. It also causes students who are not the most motivated to wait for someone to tell them what to do. If they have a specific role assigned to them, then it is no mystery as to what they should be doing. The various roles should be thought out and planned during the set-up of the project and the writing of the contract. It can be changed as the project goes along to best fit the needs of the group, but starting without established roles makes it difficult for people to know how to begin.

Having these roles clearly laid out also allows you the teacher/project manager to hold students more accountable. If a particular aspect of the project is not done, rather than blaming the entire group, you can place the accountability with the person who was responsible. This also eliminates the aspect of small-group work that many students dread; that their grade is dependent upon someone else. Many students are not comfortable with this concept and rightfully so. Students who have done their work at a high quality should not have their grade affected because someone else decided not to pull their weight. Not only that, if you dock other students for work someone else was responsible for, you are not truly assessing the skills of the individual student. A grade should be reflective of the level of skills that student has achieved on the project. The grade should not reflect the inability of someone else to get his or her work done. That should be reflected only in that person's grade.

This idea of roles is important because it accomplishes the first two requirements of achieving team member self-control as laid out in the book *Fundamentals of Project Management* (Heagncy, 2012). In order to achieve self-control, team members need:

1. A clear definition of what they are supposed to be doing, with the purpose stated

2. A personal plan for how to do the required work

3. Skills and resources adequate to the task

4. Feedback on progress that comes directly from the work itself

5. A clear definition of their authority to take corrective action when there is a deviation from the plan (pp. 114–115)

By having roles clearly defined in the contract, the first two steps of self-control are accomplished. You as the project manager must make sure Steps 3 through 5 are provided, which we will talk about in later chapters.

At Least Manage This

Students being able to work with each other in a group setting to accomplish a specific task is a very valuable skill to learn. According to Oakley, Felder, Brent, and Elhajj (2004):

> Compared to students taught traditionally, students taught in a manner that incorporates small-group learning achieve higher grades, learn at a deeper level, retain information longer, are less likely to drop out of school, acquire greater communication and

teamwork skills, and gain a better understanding of the environment in which they will be working as professionals.

(p. 9)

In order to have success in a small-group setting, the project manager must be very purposeful about teaching students how to collaborate. This can be accomplished by making sure students are aware of differences in styles of work, creating norms for how people are expected to work in groups, and making sure that roles are clear to students so they are aware of what they should be doing at all times.

Risk Management

When it is obvious that the goals cannot be reached, don't adjust the goals; adjust the action steps.

—Confucius

It would be nice to say that if you decide to use project-based learning (PBL) in your class, everything will be hunky dory and that every student who participates in projects will be a better person because of it. The reality is that like most things, there is no guarantee PBL will be successful. There are certain things you can do as the project manager though to prevent a project from failing and making sure students are getting the best education possible as a result of using PBL.

WHY PROJECTS FAIL

It is important to understand what causes a project to be unsuccessful. By understanding these, you can avoid or minimize them and ensure that you have a successful project. According to Jim Stewart (2012), the top 10 reasons projects in business fail are the following:

1. Scope creep (loss of focus)

2. Overallocated resources

3. Poor communications

4. Bad stakeholder management (too many people butting in)

5. Unreliable estimates

6. No risk management

7. Unsupported project culture

8. The accidental project manager (teacher being made to do PBL)

9. Lack of team planning sessions

10. Monitoring and controlling

These are usually the same culprits in the classroom. Most of these can be controlled by the project manager/teacher through effective monitoring and controlling. Bad stakeholder management in the school would mean you work for an administration that does not see the value of PBL and is constantly challenging you to use another method to teach students. It is important to have the support of administration. One way to ensure this is to invite them to the classroom. Have them see the wonderful things PBL has to offer students and the enduring learning that comes from it. When you have a final product due, ask administration to be your authentic audience and even to help evaluate. When they see PBL in action, they will most likely be impressed. The accidental project manager would be the exact opposite—administration wants the teacher to use PBL, but the teacher is not motivated in that technique of teaching or is not properly trained and lacks the confidence to successfully manage the classroom.

Two of the largest culprits for failed projects are scope creep and unreliable estimates. Having students set up their project using contracts helps to prevent scope creep or loss of focus. If students do not have a contract, they can often lose focus of what they are supposed to be doing or get distracted by some aspect of the project that is not as important. Having students create learning objectives for their projects as well as goals can go a long way in ensuring that students remain focused.

For instance, let us imagine that students are working on a science project dealing with the water cycle. The teacher has the following Common Core Standard

> Water moves through the water cycle in two primary ways—evaporation and condensation. This movement of water is connected to humans and human communities

(Common Core State Standards, 2014, Paragraph 5.3b).

Students have been tasked with creating a model that demonstrates the water cycle and would teach others. They can use whatever materials they like. When students are writing up the contract, they will want to be sure to include learning objectives that state what it is they are going to be learning by conducting this project. The students (with coaching of course) might create learning objectives that look like this:

- Must complete an entire cycle from beginning to end and then back around to the beginning again
- Should demonstrate the various states of water
- Water cycle should include aspects we would see in our own community
- Need to introduce something to the cycle that could alter it and discuss the long term implications

Comparing the learning objectives to the content standard, it seems obvious the content of the standard is being addressed. The part about demonstrating the various states and the one about how it looks in the community would enable students to learn what they are supposed to. In addition, the learning objectives begin at a lower level of thinking as evidenced by such verbs as *demonstrate* and *complete*, but the next two objectives are getting into higher levels of thinking, the third one connecting it to their own world, and the last one by asking students to introduce something and discuss long-term implications. This has taken it from a project where students are just learning the basics of the water cycle to actually having to think about it. This is the reason we use projects in the classroom, to achieve this level of complex and critical thinking.

Having learning objectives such as these will enable students to keep their focus and not suffer from scope creep. It would also be the task of the teacher as the project manager to check in periodically with the group to make sure they do not lose sight of these objectives. Holding students accountable to these objectives and communicating this to students is a good way to ensure that they maintain their focus.

Unreliable estimates are when a person working on the project under-estimates how much time it is going to take to accomplish a task. She may have allotted herself two weeks when realistically it would probably take a month. Students especially have a habit of biting off more than they can chew and then realize it too late before they can adjust. As a result, they produce a product that is not of the highest quality. Again, the project contract will help a lot with this. If the teacher sees what the product is going to be, he can make sure it is a realistic one. Another way to help with unreliable estimates is the use of a project calendar. This can come in a couple of forms. The first is the use of a classroom calendar. Having a calendar that plots out the long-term project and checkpoints for where they should be can be displayed for all of the class to see. Figure 6.1 is an example of such a calendar.

Figure 6.1   Classroom Calendar

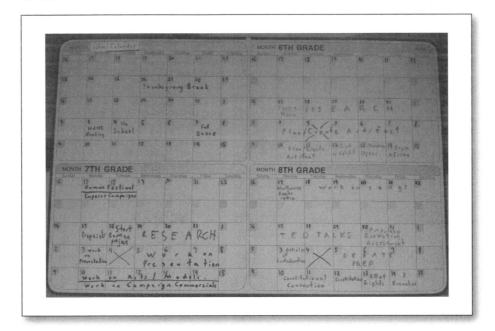

This is a PBL teacher that teaches multiple grade levels, so there is a need for three different calendars. In addition, the two seventh-grade classes are actually working on separate projects. The top project is for one class of students while the bottom for another. In the upper-left section is the school calendar to inform students of possible events that could affect the project such as days off or meetings. Having such a calendar gives a visual reminder to students where they are in the project, how far they still have to go, and where they should be. It allows students who need things broken down to see the individual pieces, but also the big picture so one can see how it looks when it is all put together.

A teacher could also provide individual calendars for students. If students are working on different projects with different criteria and due dates, this individual calendar will allow the students to make sure they are where they need to be. This calendar would be created by the student and referred to when going over the contract and conducting conferences. It might look something like this:

Student Name: Jenny

Name of Project: Shaking up Shakespeare

Due Date of Project: Friday October 27

Day 1	Day 2	Day 3	Day 4	Day 5
Begin reading *The Taming of the Shrew*	Continue reading *The Taming of the Shrew*	Continue reading *The Taming of the Shrew*	Continue reading *The Taming of the Shrew*	Finish reading *The Taming of the Shrew*
Day 6	Day 7	Day 8	Day 9	Day 10
Write analysis of universal themes	Write analysis of universal themes	Write analysis of universal themes	Write analysis of universal themes	Watch movie *10 Things I Hate About You*
Day 11	Day 12	Day 13	Day 14	Day 15
Create film trailer comparing the two	Create film trailer comparing the two	Create film trailer comparing the two	Create film trailer comparing the two	Finish film trailer comparing the two
Day 16	Day 17	Day 18	Day 19	Day 20
Presentation Day				

This is a project where different students are reading different plays and watching different movies so each student might need a calendar specific to him or her. The final product was also a choice, and this student chose to film a trailer that compares the play and film. Another student's calendar might reflect a different product.

HEADING OFF PROBLEMS

The issues of poor communication, unsupported project culture, and lack of team planning sessions can all be tackled with the use of conferences/ reviews. As the project manager, you need to develop a delicate balance of giving your students enough space to allow them to create wonderful products, but at the same time, making sure they are not going to crash and burn. A good way to accomplish this is through the use of conferences/reviews. There are three types of reviews that can be conducted with students:

- Status reviews
- Process reviews
- Design reviews (Heagney, 2012, p. 119)

Status reviews are basically maintenance reviews, checking in with the group and making sure they are where they need to be in regard to the calendar and deadlines. This involves the teacher and students sitting down with the calendar and seeing where exactly the group is. For example, if the group has been allotted a week for research purposes yet when the teacher conducts the status review in the middle of the week, it turns out the members do not have many notes. This is where the project manager tries to right the ship and get the group back on track. He may suggest checking in the following day to be sure they are making better progress, and this accountability will motivate the group to get more research done than the pace they had originally set. On the opposite side are those groups that are ahead of the schedule. Take the same project with a week of research and when the teacher checks in with the group halfway through the week, they have already gotten most of what they need. They could move on to the next part of the project that will give them more time to create a quality product, or they could take a day to go over their notes and organize them in a way that will allow them to use them more effectively in the product. As the project manager in the classroom, you do not want people finishing projects at different times although this is bound to happen because students work at different paces. The task of the project manager/teacher is to challenge those students who do finish early to improve the quality of the product. This does not mean giving them extra work (students hate nothing more than that), but it simply means having them analyze their product and ensuring it meets all the criteria of the project at a high-quality level. Students could take the rubric out and check over all aspects to make sure they have been met. It is these adjustments to projects that turn a good project into a great one. Helping students to achieve this and realize that just completing the project is not the goal, but rather, it is to produce the best quality product within the time allotted. That means if there is additional time, finding ways to improve the product.

Status reviews need not be formal. It could simply be the teacher verbally checking with the group to see how things are going or through observation knowing where a group is at (the teacher could even use the one page project manager sheet for this). For groups a teacher notices are not where they should be, some encouragement and motivation might be necessary. There should be at least one formal status review a week, preferably in the middle of the week, so that students do not get too far behind. These can be scheduled just as a meeting in the business world would be, having students sign up for appointments and putting the meetings on the calendar.

Process reviews are less about management of time and more about producing a high-quality product. In *Fundamentals of Project Management*, it is suggested that process reviews ask two questions:

1. What have we done well so far?

2. What do we want to improve for the future? (Heagney, 2012, p. 122)

Whereas a status review is just an eyeball check to make sure the car is going in the correct direction, a process check is actually opening up the hood and taking a good look at whether the engine is running well. These meetings ideally would be held at the end of a work week or the first day in the next work week to reflect upon what students have to work toward their project. If students are spending the week conducting research, the teacher and students will sit down together and talk about the notes that were taken, what was learned from them, and how these can be applied to the final product. If students have been building a model, this would mean analyzing the model, comparing it to the rubric to ensure that the learning outcomes are being addressed. Depending how long the project is, these should be scheduled periodically no longer than a week between. This gives students enough time to work independently and find what it is they need but also catches any potential problems before it gets too far.

In these meetings, the teacher can ask the group to evaluate the quality of their project at that point in time. If it is not where it needs to be, then what needs to change in their efforts and work in order to achieve that higher quality of product? This will require students to have some self-reflection skills, but with the project manager/teacher directing them, they should be able to identify what their next steps will be to improve the project.

Design reviews in the business world mean if a project involves designing hardware/software, a campaign, or a specific product, does that look like the group intended it to and does it accomplish what it is supposed to? In the case of the classroom, this is the teacher/project manager carving out some time for students to be able to evaluate the final product before its due date. For example, if the product for a language arts project is a performance, is there an opportunity for the students to give a preview performance to an outside evaluator to catch any mistakes or issues the group might have overlooked? This gives the group a chance to have someone use the rubric to see how well their performance accomplishes what the rubric is asking. Or if a student produces a math portfolio, having someone take a look at it to evaluate its quality and offer suggestions for improvement. These design reviews can be set up by the teacher in a couple of different ways.

The first way is giving students the time to conduct these design reviews. That might mean dedicating an entire class or two to allowing students to share with other groups their product and to get feedback or arranging for a study hall or other class to come in as an impartial audience who can offer feedback on a product. It can be as simple as having students swap papers and conducting a peer review, but there should be structure to this so that the feedback is meaningful. Having the outside evaluator use the rubric would be the best way to offer feedback, but an additional peer review could be created (there is an example of a peer review in the Reproducibles section).

A second way to conduct design reviews is to partner students up with someone who has an expertise and can offer more meaningful advice. What this might look like is if students are writing a memoir for their literature class, partnering that student up with a professional writer willing to give some time to advise the student throughout the process and to review the final product. This person acts as a mentor to the student and provides an expertise maybe even the teacher does not possess. Or if in a science class students are designing an engineering product, actually connecting them with an engineer who can provide valuable insight. It does not even need to be a so-called expert. If students are working in Social Studies on a personal budget where they must create a portfolio of their monthly expenses and the choices they made as a result, they could go over this portfolio with their parents who could offer insight about the family budget and the choices they have to make.

Design reviews are basically a rough draft or a rehearsal before the final performance to make sure issues are ironed out and that students are producing the highest quality product they can.

HANDLING THE UNMOTIVATED

If you have not figured out by now, working on projects takes a lot of self-discipline. Because of this, those students who have difficulty getting motivated can be a challenge working in small groups. Much of this lack of motivation can be eliminated by the fact you are using PBL. Because there is more choice with PBL than other types of learning, students tend to be more motivated because they have some say in how they are going to be learning. Additional motivation can come from the peer reviews that accompany projects. Knowing that fellow students, a group who opinions a student might be more concerned with than the teacher's, are going to be judging and evaluating his actions might cause a student to become more motivated not because of his own grade, but because his actions might affect the work of others and that will not be socially acceptable.

Even offering all of these wonderful choices and making them accountable to group mates, some students might continue to be unmotivated. If you have a student who is chronically unmotivated when working on projects to the point where she is affecting the groups she works with, the best solution is to offer an alternative to the project. If the class is conducting a research experiment concerning chemical reactions and have been tasked with an experiment of their own design and undertaking, could that same learning be provided to the unmotivated student in another form whether it be a textbook, online seminar, or having a more structured experiment for her to follow? If it could, offer this alternative to the unmotivated student.

Participating in PBL should be viewed as a privilege for students, and because it is a privilege, it is one that can be taken away if students are not using it to their advantage or are unwilling to participate fully. You should not offer this alternative to a student after one failed project. The student should display a pattern of undesired motivation toward projects before this option is used, but for some students, the alternative plays more into their strengths or avoids their weaknesses. A student sitting down at a desk reading through a textbook and answering review questions at the end of the chapter might be the structure the student needs in order to be successful. As wonderful as it would be to think that PBL is great for all students, there are those it does not work well for. Having a plan B to help these students in their learning is always a wise idea.

RISK MANAGEMENT

The logical question is why take a risk in the first place? The reason is that the most innovative products ever created were risks. Apple takes risks with its products such as the iPad and iPhone. Amazon constantly is taking risks, expanding into self-publishing and even creating their own television shows rather than just selling other people's. Student projects that have the greatest impact are usually the ones where the students took a risk. Sometimes these risks resulted in an inferior product because students either bit off more than they could chew or lost sight of their scope. Other times the end product displayed an amazing amount of depth and had a far-reaching lesson beyond the content you wanted students to learn.

Like most things in life, there is a fine line in this risk. You as the project manager/teacher have to allow students the opportunity to take a risk but not to the point where they are in danger of failing. Figure 6.2 shows what the levels of learning look like.

Figure 6.2   Targets of Learning

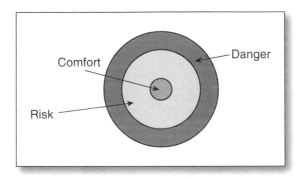

In the comfort level at the center, there is not much learning going on. Learners are covering things they possibly already know, and although it feels good, they are not getting much out of it. On the outer edge of learning is the danger zone. If you put learners in a place they are so unfamiliar they are fearful of it, they will shut down, and no learning will occur. Learners have to walk the precarious tightrope of the risk zone. Learners must be challenged, feeling a little uncomfortable, but not so much they are in danger. That is the optimal place for learning to take place. PBL certainly provides this risk zone, especially if students are used to a more traditional way of learning. It also can cause students to enter the danger zone a lot easier than the traditional classroom.

As the project manager/teacher, your job is to navigate students through the risk zone, keeping them challenged and learning new things, without going too far and entering the danger zone. One way to avoid the danger zone is to consider the possible sources of risk. Here is a list adapted from Richman in *Improving Your Project Management Skills* (2012):

- Technical
- Administrative
- Environmental
- Resource availability
- Human
- Logistical (p. 164)

Most of these risk factors can be avoided by an observant project manager/teacher. *Technical* concerns whether students have the skills in order to achieve their product. In other words, if you have required them to create a Prezi, do students have the training and knowledge to use that piece of technology to create their product? It is also about providing resources. If you are asking students to research databases, you need to either provide them time in the computer lab or have a classroom set of laptops that they can access the information. *Administrative* is whether you the teacher, the administrator of the project, are giving your students the support they need to accomplish the project but at the same time, providing enough space where they feel they can work without being interrupted by too many deadlines, check-ins, or busy work. This will be discussed in more detail later in the book. *Environmental* is setting up the best atmosphere for students to be able to work on their projects with much success. The way you set up your classroom from the desks and chairs to the resources and mood can go a long way in ensuring the success of students working on independent projects. *Resource availability* is whether students have the resources needed to create an innovative product. That might mean access to technology, experts, books, etc. *Human risk* comes down to the people you are working with. In a group, is everyone on the same page and moving in the same direction toward the group goals? The creation of group norms and the performance reviews where students conduct peer evaluations go a long way in ensuring that the people in the group are doing what they are supposed to be doing. The teacher as the project manager also has a lot of influence on keeping students on task and contributing to their projects. *Logistical* comes down to the project design itself, or what lesson plan did the teacher create. Is it clear to students what the expectations are? Has the final product been demonstrated for students so they have a clear idea of what they are to be producing? Is the timeline the teacher has set out realistic for students to be able to complete their project in a timely fashion? Like any lesson, the teacher will want to reflect upon the process with the class and discuss what worked and what could be improved for next time. You as the teacher are certainly taking a risk with a new project where you do not know exactly how things are going to turn out because you have no past experiences to go on. But this risk is well worth it when students create amazing products that teach at a far deeper level than traditional methods.

More than anything a project manager needs to be open minded to the ideas and innovations of students and be willing to allow them to take a risk. If a student wants to try something different than what was prescribed by the teacher, would you be willing to let them attempt this as long as the learning objectives were learned by the student?

At Least Manage This

Projects fail for a whole assortment of reasons. It is your responsibility as the project manager of your classroom to help students to avoid the pitfalls of what makes a project fail and at the same time, keep them in the risk zone so the products they are creating are innovative and result in a deeper-level learning. The more preparation that is done before the beginning of the project the less likely something will go wrong. The teacher needs to be sure these expectations are communicated clearly so that students know where they need to go and what risks they can take.

Different Types of Products

7

*If you can't describe what you are doing as a process, you don't know
what you're doing.*

—W. Edwards Deming

At this point, you might be wondering to yourself, "This all sounds
very well and good and seems to have sound theory behind it, but
what the heck does this thing actually look like?" The good news is that
this chapter intends to show you the possibilities of assessment in a 21st
century project-based learning (PBL) classroom through different types of
products. There are literally thousands of possibilities for a product in
regard to PBL, but for the benefit of this chapter, we will focus on 10 basic
performance assessments that can be accomplished through PBL and the
advantages of each.

- Presentation
- Museum/exhibit
- Debate
- Performance
- Competition
- Portfolio
- Research paper

- Model
- Technology-driven products
- Entrepreneurship

All of these products can be taken in hundreds of different directions, but the basic idea will be laid out for each as well as the 21st century skill it best teaches.

PRESENTATION

This is the most obvious of performance assessments, when a student or group of students get in front of the class and must give an oral presentation on some subject in order to show what he has learned. If done right, these sorts of presentations also allow the audience to learn. There can be all sorts of bells and whistles added to a presentation such as visual aids, skits, interacting with the audience, conducting a fish bowl interview, and various others. The general idea is that students are taking what they have learned and synthesizing it into verbal form, then sharing this with others.

It is even better when you can have students giving presentations that would benefit them in the business world. Gaining experience on presenting a product or trying to persuade someone of something are valuable skills for students to possess. Here are some examples of these types of presentations as provided by Harvard Business School (2007):

- **Sales**: Outlines the benefits, features, and reasons to buy a product or service
- **Persuasion**: Provides the reasons or support to pursue a particular idea or path
- **Status report**: Details the progress of a project, a task force, or product sales
- **Product demonstration**: Shows how something works
- **Business plan or strategy**: Sketches out what an organization plans to do next, or articulates the company's goals

Using these types of presentations with students allows them to gain experience in something they might see in the real world. You could use a persuasion presentation to convince the audience of themes in a book, in science class students could build a bridge and then give a product demonstration of it, a math class might come up with a business plan analyzing an existing company or creating one of their own and discussing budgets, finances, and expenditures, and so on.

The obvious 21st century skill is effective oral communication. A presentation requires that students share their information orally and must figure out the most effective way to do so. Think of it like an essay question only the student gets to express herself through oral communication rather than written. Another obvious benefit of such a product is building confidence in students to publically speak. Some students are painfully shy and would rather walk on hot coals than have to present in front of their peers or strangers. However, the more experience they gain in public speaking, the less apprehensive they are about it. This is a skill that any business would want of their employees from the CEO of Microsoft to the cashier taking your order at McDonalds.

MUSEUM/EXHIBIT

It seems that it becomes more and more difficult to arrange fieldtrips. From the cost of busses, to the arranging of chaperones, to figuring out all the medical supplies you have to bring, the prospect of actually getting out to a museum is not good. Not only that, you might not have a museum in your community that has an exhibit that ties in with the content you teach. The solution is fairly simple: create your own museum.

What this looks like is the teacher chooses a theme of the museum. Let us say a social studies teacher has a unit on Egypt, and she wants to emphasize how important the Nile was to the formation and growth of that civilization. The theme could be: How did the Nile River affect Egyptian culture?

Students then could choose topics from the Egyptians they would like to learn more about such as pharaohs, mummification, pyramids, gods and goddesses, etc. Students would then be charged with creating a museum exhibit that has both a student-created artifact and a display that would teach someone about this aspect of Egyptian culture, making sure somewhere in the exhibit to discuss the ties to the river and how the river shaped this aspect of culture. A student might choose mummification and then show the various stages of the process with seven different dolls, taking us from the initial removal of organs to the wrapping of the body. The display, either a poster board or a trifold, would contain additional information explaining the process in detail (to see an example of an Egyptian museum go to the website http://resources.corwin.com/StanleyCreatingLearners).

With each student or groups of students creating exhibits, you can put them all on display in a room, cafeteria, or auditorium and invite other classes to partake in the museum as well as inviting parents and community members. This makes the project more real as students must create an exhibit not just for the sake of their own grade, but for others to be able to learn.

The 21st century skill this best captures is accessing and analyzing information. Although the product is a visual one, students must synthesize information they get through research to display on their board as well as choose an artifact that truly shows how this aspect was used by the Egyptians. In the example of mummification, it is not just a student wrapping a Barbie doll in toilet paper. It is using a variety of dolls to show the various stages of the mummification process, allowing those viewing to learn about the process. Students must also make a connection to the river, requiring them to analyze their information and draw a conclusion.

DEBATE

The idea of debate is to find a topic that does not have an easy answer and allowing two students or groups of students to argue for one of the sides against the other. For example, in language arts the class is reading the book *A Lesson before Dying* by Ernest Gaines. This novel, about an educated black man in the 1940s who befriends a death row inmate and tries to instill in him how to have pride, has a lot of themes that are debatable. Is there such thing as dying with pride? Is the death penalty fair? Can a black man in the 1940s receive a fair trial in the South? Is it more important to learn about religion and have faith than to receive a college education?

The class could be split into two sides, one arguing the affirmative, the other the negative. Students must use examples from the book to back their arguments as well as any additional research. The students would be provided a debate format and have to construct their arguments accordingly. A debate format is necessary to give the students some structure to follow. If you simply stated, "I want you to debate one another," it will turn into more of an argument than a debate. The format does not need to be overly detailed but should give the students some idea of what their final debate needs to look like. Here is an example of one such debate format:

Cross-Examination Format

Time assigned to each section can be decided on by the teacher.

1. Affirmative opening argument

2. Team conference

3. Negative cross-examination

    a. One person asking questions
    b. One person answering questions

4. Negative opening argument

5. Team conference

6. Affirmative cross-examination

   a. One person asking question
   b. One person answering questions

7. Team conference

8. Affirmative closing argument

9. Negative closing argument

Through these debates students have to cite evidence in order to make their arguments stronger and depending on the format, must think quickly on their feet in order to create counterarguments and rebuttals. Because of this, the 21st century skill this best accomplishes is adaptability.

PERFORMANCE

Performance can be in many different forms, but essentially, it involves a student playing a role and by putting himself in the shoes of this person or character, learning something about the situation at a deeper level. For example, a science teacher wants to look at creationism versus evolution and the debate that rages between the two. In order to teach this to the class through performance, the teacher could conduct a mock trial of the Scopes Monkey Trial. The class would have to research the trial itself and create a list of witnesses for both the prosecution and the defense who will testify to the respective sides. There would be lawyers who play William Jennings Bryan and Clarence Darrow, the famous men who acted as attorneys in the trial. The teacher could even run two trials, one from the perspective of the 1920s when it originally took place, and one from the perspective of present day to reflect changes that have happened over the past century.

Performance can also be plays, filming commercials, giving speeches for a presidential campaign, a living wax museum, and other such products. The 21st century skill this type of product best teaches is effective oral communication. Because the students are playing a role, they must effectively find a way to communicate their part verbally to allow others to learn from it.

COMPETITION

Nothing brings out motivation in students more than being involved in a competition. From the earliest competition of spelling bees and science fairs, students like to compete against one another. If you can arrange a classroom project where you pit students against one another, the competitiveness of the students usually results in high-quality projects, trying to outdo one another.

For example, in math class, you give an engineering design challenge. Students must design a city to scale, having correct measurements for what the city's dimensions are in real life. There could be other mathematical formulas needed for the model such as how many gallons of water the sewage system can hold, the cost of repairs to roads and parks, the perimeter of the city grids, surface area, coordinates, point plotting and angles with buildings, etc. The cities will be judged on their innovative use of environmental friendly technology, the creativity of the models, and of course whether the math is correct. One city will be picked as the one the teacher or the panel of judges would most want to live in.

If you are able to connect with a state or national competition, that just brings even more legitimacy to the project. For example, the above project could be connected to Future Cities Competition.

> The Future City Competition is a national, project-based learning experience where students in 6th, 7th, and 8th grade imagine, design, and build cities of the future. Students work as a team with an educator and engineer mentor to plan cities using Sim-City™ software; research and write solutions to an engineering problem; build tabletop scale models with recycled materials; and present their ideas before judges at Regional Competitions in January. Regional winners represent their region at the National Finals in Washington, DC, in February.
>
> (National Engineers Week, 2011)

Usually with state or national competitions, there are outside evaluators and stronger competition, resulting in an even higher quality of work. There are National Competitions for language arts (WordMasters, Promising Young Writers Program, National Peace Essay); science (Robotics, Invent America, Science Olympiad); math (Mathcounts, American Mathematics Competition, USA Mathematical Talent Search); and social studies (Model United Nations, National Current Events League, National Geography Challenge), as well as general competitions that promote higher levels of thinking and problem solving such as Destination Imagination, Odyssey of the Mind, and Future Problem Solvers (Karnes & Riley, 2005).

The 21st century skill that competition best brings out is collaboration across networks. This comes in the fact that many of these competitions are organized in teams so students must learn to collaborate with one another in order to be successful. Even the competitions where students are working by themselves, they are exposed to others' ideas at the competition and may even have the opportunity to network with peers from other parts of the state and nation.

PORTFOLIO

A portfolio is a collection of work. There are two types of portfolios: a process and a product. A process portfolio shows the evolution of student work. In math class, a student might include a work example from the beginning of the year, the middle, and the end and then reflect how they have grown mathematically over the course of the year, what can they do that they could not before, and how have they been able to apply what they have learned in math to other aspects of life. A product portfolio demonstrates mastery of learning objectives either set by the teacher or student (Venn, 2000, p. 533). In science, this might be looking at learning objectives such as the following:

- Describe the role of producers in the transfer of energy entering ecosystems as sunlight to chemical energy through photosynthesis.
- Explain how almost all kinds of animals' food can be traced back to plants.
- Trace the organization of simple food chains and food webs (e.g., producers, herbivores, carnivores, omnivores, and decomposers).
- Summarize that organisms can survive only in ecosystems in which their needs can be met (e.g., food, water, shelter, air, carrying capacity and waste disposal). The world has different ecosystems and distinct ecosystems support the lives of different types of organisms.

The student would then produce original work that addresses these learning objectives or find other work that demonstrates them with student commentary and reflection of what was learned.

Online portfolios are another way students can demonstrate learning through a portfolio. What an online portfolio looks like according to the Glossary of Education Reform is:

Portfolios may be digital collections or presentations that include the documents and achievements, but that may also include additional content such as student-created videos, multimedia presentations, spreadsheets, websites, photographs, or other digital artifacts of learning . . . online journals may be maintained by students and include ongoing reflections related to learning activities and progress.

(Great Schools Partnerships, 2013)

This allows students use of technology as well as making easier additions and editing to the portfolio.

The 21st century skill being addressed with portfolios due to the amount of reflection required is critical thinking and problem solving. Students must think critically about their progress over the course of the portfolio as well as create ways for improvement and future goals. If the portfolio is a product one, students are using problem-solving skills to determine how best to answer or show they understand the learning objectives.

RESEARCH PAPER

A research paper is more than just a book report. A research paper has many steps before even getting to the writing aspect of the project including researching, synthesizing information, drawing conclusions, and making evaluations based on evidence. Then there is the writing aspect of it, organizing the paper to make it coherent, citing sources, being grammatically correct with spelling and punctuation, and creating a references/bibliography. The number of topics a research paper could be used for are unlimited. Math could write research papers about innovative mathematical accomplishments and their impact on the world, science could research various theories, how they came about, and how thinking was changed as a result, social studies could conduct research papers on a particular era of time such as westward expansion or investigating a career the student is interested in, and language arts could look at biographies, comparison of an author's body of work, an analysis of themes, and so on.

And research papers can be used for multiple disciplines. The science teacher could grade the paper based on the accuracy and insight about the given topic, the social studies teacher could look at the history of the concept as well as references and citing sources, while the language arts teacher could focus on the sentence structure and professionalism of the writing. One research paper could produce multiple assessments in multiple subject areas, all focusing on a different aspect of the paper.

Written communication is the most prevalent 21st century skill being assessed by such a product. There are others as well, including critical thinking and accessing and analyzing information, which is what makes it such a good product for students to create.

MODEL

The use of models in PBL is probably the one that results in the most failed products. The reason why is often times students stop at the model. In other words, they create the model, but there is no clear evidence of learning other than the fact that the model represents something about the topic they were supposed to learn about and usually only at a surface level. An example would be in social studies, if students were studying Roman culture, a student team produces a model of the Coliseum complete with trap doors, scaled to model, and even participants competing in the arena. The question is though what is such a product teaching about Roman culture other than the fact they had a Coliseum? There needs to be more substance to the product. The model typically serves as the visual aid, and the students must provide additional information either in the form of an oral explanation, labels, a trifold with information, an analysis of the model, or something else that demonstrates a deeper understanding.

What this might look like in science class is giving students a design challenge where they must create a better mousetrap. Students must design and create a model of a working mousetrap. The improvement they must make from the original mousetrap is their trap cannot harm the mouse in any way. This project is not just about the model. The students would need to demonstrate how the mousetrap works without harming the mouse as well as writing an analysis comparing their mousetrap with the original, discussing advantages and disadvantages of both as well as making an argument for which of the mousetraps is better (for a copy of this project look in the Reproducibles section).

A model demonstrates many things, but the 21st century skills it mostly reflects are critical thinking and problem solving. When students create a model, they usually have to figure out how to construct it and at the same time, have it reflect what has been learned. This is not as simple as creating a house out of popsicle sticks or building a baking soda volcano. Students must think critically how their model should be constructed and what it should represent as well as problem solve the design challenge of what materials to use and how to construct it.

TECHNOLOGY-DRIVEN PRODUCTS

Technology is a wonderful thing. It can accentuate a presentation to make it more interactive and visually stimulating, but many fall into the trap of thinking technology will do everything for us. Does a student need to create a PowerPoint presentation or would having them draw it on a poster board be just as if not more effective? Technology is supposed to be a tool, not the end all be all. Teachers need to consider when they are asking for a technology-driven product the reasoning behind using the technology and the rationale for what it teaches.

There are several good technology-driven products that can be used in the classroom to demonstrate learning. Because technology is moving at such a rapid pace, creating a list of technology examples would be moot because probably by the time it took to write this sentence to when it was published and in your hands, the technology has become obsolete. It is important as a teacher to stay informed and up to date of various technology that can be used in the classroom as well as being open-minded about incorporating it into projects.

A simple example would be using podcasts to have students show what they have learned. In a social studies class where they are studying the River Valley Civilizations of Ancient Mesopotamia, India, and China, their assignment would look like this:

INTEROFFICE MEMORANDUM

SUBJECT

The River Valley Civilizations

PURPOSE

We have been hired to create mini podcasts that teachers can have students listen to that teach them about a certain topic. The topic we have been hired to teach is the River Valley Civilizations.

SUMMARY

Mesopotamia, China, and India all began to develop near major rivers. These were the first major civilizations. You are to pick an aspect of one of the three cultures and conduct more in depth research, learning everything you can about it. You will then turn this information into a podcast that would teach someone listening about the topic.

DISCUSSION

- Why was the river essential to the survival of these civilizations?
- How did the river shape the culture of these civilizations?
- Would this civilization have been able to survive without the presence of a river?

RECOMMENDATION

You must create a podcast that will teach listeners about the topic you have chosen. The podcast must be 10 to 15 minutes long. The podcast will be evaluated in three areas:

- Content
- Clarity
- Connection to the river

You will start by gaining a basic understanding of the culture of Mesopotamia, China, and India.

Students have to create a 10- to 15-minute long podcast that answers the learning objectives the students have created for their rubric. A student contract might look like this:

PROJECT CONTRACT

Student(s) Name: Grace M., Marina S., Kane C., Maddie M.

Project Topic: Chinese Gender Roles

Essential Question: How does it connect to river?

Due Date of Project: September 19

Learning Outcomes *(At least three):*

1. How were woman treated in ancient China? Why were they treated this way?

(Continued)

(Continued)

2. How were man treated in ancient China? Why were they treated this way?

3. How does the river influence gender roles in ancient China?

Group Goal (s): Finish the project by deadline and get an excellent evaluation_____

_____

_____

Product of Project: Interview podcast, Maddie & Kane: Male research; Marina & Grace: Female research

_____

_____

Student(s) Signature:

Grace Marman_____

Marina Saunders_____

Kane Cabel_____

Maddie Martin_____

Teacher Signature: _____

Students then must create a podcast that answers the learning objectives in the allotted time (for an example of such a podcast, go to the website http://resources.corwin.com/StanleyCreatingLearners). They must conduct research and figure out how to convey this information in their audio presentation. By having this form of technology, students must figure out without visuals how to best teach the class about their topic. The technology is forcing them to consider how they are going to teach it in the most effective manner possible. The rubric used to evaluate this product might look like this:

Podcast Lesson

Student(s) _____ Cultural Aspect _____

Overall	Clarity	Connection to the River	Content
Excellent (A)	• The podcast can be clearly heard through the entire broadcast, and the participants speak slowly and clearly during the duration. • The information being given is clearly conveyed and the person listening can understand what the podcast is trying to teach them. • The podcast is organized in a manner that makes it easy to follow and understand what is going on at any given time.	• There is a clear connection made between this aspect of culture and the river. • Student explains with examples how the river shaped this particular aspect of culture. • The connection to river is a deep one that explores many aspects rather than just a surface level comparison.	• Aspect of culture is explained in detail. • There is obvious research in the content, teaching the reader how they used this aspect of culture. • Podcast teaches the listener for 10 to 15 minutes.
Good (B–C)	• The podcast can be clearly heard for most of the broadcast, and the participants speak slowly and clearly during a majority of the duration, but there are a couple of spots where it is difficult to hear. • The information being given is clearly conveyed for the most part, and the persons listening can understand what the podcast is trying to teach them, but there is time where there is some confusion caused by the speakers. • The podcast is organized in a manner that makes it easy to follow and understand what is going on at any given time.	• There is a connection between this aspect of culture and the river, but it is not as clear as could be. • Student explains how the river shaped this particular aspect of culture but does not provide clear examples. • The connection to river explores a couple of aspects but does not go into the depth that it could have.	• Aspect of culture is explained but lacks detail in places where it is needed. • There is a little research in the content, but does not clearly teach the reader how they used this aspect of culture. • Podcast teaches the listener for 8 to 9 minutes.

(Continued)

(Continued)

| Needs Improvement (D–F) | • The podcast cannot be heard for a good portion of the broadcast, and/or the participants do not speak slowly and clearly during the duration making it difficult to understand what they are saying.

• The information being given is not clearly conveyed, and the person listening has difficulty understanding what the podcast is trying to teach.

• The podcast is not very organized, making it difficult to follow and understand what is going on at any given time. | • There is not a connection made between this aspect of culture and the river.

• Student does not explain how the river shaped this particular aspect of culture or explains incorrectly.

• The connection to river is a surface level one that does not really indicate how this aspect of culture was influenced by the presence of the river. | • Aspect of culture is not well explained, causing confusion.

• There is no research in the content, failing to teach the reader how they used this aspect of culture.

• Podcast only teaches for 6 minutes or less. |

The 21st century skill best learned in this type of product would be curiosity and imagination. The technology is merely a means to convey student curiosity, and if a teacher is using technology, it should allow students to use their imagination to make it a much stronger product. Students can use technology to create amazing products. You as the project manager just need to give them the proper guidance to use it to its fullest potential.

ENTREPRENEURSHIP

This involves students actually selling, marketing, and/or planning their product. This would have students putting into practice rather than theory, making the learning authentic and the lessons more meaningful. It would mean students actively involved with the selling of the product and experiencing the interactive nature such a lesson has to offer.

A teacher could have an interdisciplinary unit using this sort of product such as The Lemonade Stand project:

THE LEMONADE STAND

Project Description

Businesses are formed in order to sell products or services to make a profit for the person owning the business. They also provide valuable products or services that the public may need. There are many businesses in the city that do this very thing.

If you were to sell a product in our school, what would you start and why? Who would be your target customer? What are some things you could do to ensure success and avoid failure? How would you advertise for your product? Why would people buy your product or services over others?

You will be divided into teams. These three teams will create a business plan in which they will come up with a product to sell in the cafeteria during lunch. Each team will be selling so there will be competition for the goods and services you might be offering. In addition, you will have to create an advertising campaign so that your target customer is aware of your product and would be willing to buy it.

SOCIAL STUDIES PRODUCT—BUSINESS PLAN

Explain that individuals in all economies must answer the fundamental economic questions of what to produce, how to produce, and for whom to produce. Also include where you would have your business and why.

- Scarce goods
- Specialization
- Interdependent
- Supply and demand
- Competitive market
- Competition

LANGUAGE ARTS PRODUCT— ADVERTISING CAMPAIGN

Advertising: You will create a 1- to 3-minute commercial where you combine all these items together, who and what you are selling, at what price, and against what competition. You also must produce posters, write announcements, and create any other marketing tools you would need to sell your product.

MATH PRODUCT—POLLING/ACCOUNTING

- Using probability to predict what customers would like in a product.
- Polling potential customers to see what they would be interested in.
- Estimating both costs and expenses as compared to potential profit.
- Accurately keeping track of sales and profits.

The final product students are actually selling in the cafeteria. To make it more like capitalism, make it a competition. Just like the real world, whichever group makes the most profit (amount of money made minus cost of production) is the winner. What could be more 21st century skill than that? In fact, one of the seven survival skills is initiative and entrepreneurialism, which this product falls under quite nicely.

At Least Manage This

Using the types of products mentioned in this chapter will allow you to teach many 21st century skills to your students:

- Critical thinking and problem solving (Model, Portfolio)
- Collaboration across networks (Competition)
- Agility and adaptability (Debate)
- Initiative and entrepreneurialism (Entrepreneurship)
- Effective oral and written communication (Research paper, Performance)
- Accessing and analyzing information (Museum)
- Curiosity and imagination (Technology driven products)

It is important as the project manager that you match the correct product with the correct project in order to allow students to produce a high-quality work that requires higher-level thinking. This might involve trial and error as you are trying to figure out what works best, but one thing is for certain: by having students create products such as this, the level of learning in your classroom will be that much higher.

Assessment of the Product

All assessment is a perpetual work in progress.

—Linda Suske

Once you choose the product, you must also choose how to assess that product. Most of the products in a project-based learning (PBL) environment are performance assessments. This means they cannot be graded as one would a traditional assessment with an objective right or wrong answer. There is a certain amount of subjectivity and opinion that goes into the grade. With subjectivity and opinion of course comes its ugly step-brother, bias. This bias can prevent students from receiving a valid and reliable grade. The best way to combat this bias is by creating valid and reliable rubrics to evaluate your performance assessments.

USE OF RUBRICS

The definition of a rubric in the book *Scoring Rubrics in the Classroom* (Arter & McTighe, 2001) is "a particular format for criteria—it is the written-down version of the criteria, with all score points described and defined" (p. 8). The authors go on further to describe the qualities of a good rubric:

> The best rubrics are worded in a way that covers the essence of what we, as teachers, look for when we're judging quality, and they reflect the best thinking in the field as to what constitutes good performance. Rubrics are frequently accompanied by examples (anchors) of products or performances to illustrate the various score points on the scale.
>
> (p. 8)

There are many benefits to using rubrics, but for our purposes, we will focus on three of them. The first is a rubric allows for consistency in scoring. This helps to solve some of the problem of performance-based assessment scoring being subjective. A well-written rubric that clearly defines the criteria makes it easier for a teacher to be objective in the way he or she scores a student. Conversely, a poorly written rubric allows for much subjectivity. This is why it is so important to start with a well-written rubric.

The second benefit of a well-written rubric is that it clarifies for students the expectations of the assessment. The rubric acts as a blueprint for students. If they follow this blueprint step by step, it guarantees them a good grade. It is when they try to do things without consulting the blueprint they end up losing points. Because of this, it is always a good idea to give students the rubric for the project at the very beginning. This should inform all of their decisions. If students are using a rubric correctly, they would have it out during all portions of the creation of that product, making sure they are following the expectations laid out for an excellent result. A student should not be seeing a rubric for the first time when he or she is receiving the summative grade. The student should be aware of the expectations from the very beginning.

The third benefit of the use of rubrics is that they clarify the expectations for the teacher. You would think this would be a given for educators, but sometimes the teacher is not completely clear what he is trying to accomplish with a project. When this happens, you get a mixed bag of results because the students are not quite sure where to go because the teacher is not quite sure where he is taking them. More often than not the results are uneven. Creating rubrics clarifies for you, the teacher, what it is you are hoping for students to achieve on this assessment. This focuses your own teaching because you now know where to lead the students.

CREATING YOUR RUBRICS

What is the best way to create a rubric that is both valid and reliable? The best piece of advice on this matter is the following three words: Keep it simple. Creating a rubric is not a terribly difficult task, but it can be. If you follow some basic rules and keep it simple though, rubrics do not have to be a daunting task.

There are some basic parameters to think about when creating your rubric. Herman, Aschbacher, and Winters (1992) distinguish the following elements of a scoring rubric:

- One or more traits or dimensions that serve as the basis for judging the student response
- Definitions and examples to clarify the meaning of each trait or dimension
- A scale of values on which to rate each dimension
- Standards of excellence for specified performance levels accompanied by models or examples of each level

What that essentially means is this (a full size version of this can be found in the Reproducibles):

Figure 8.1 is the basic template for any rubric you create. It has a spot for the stated objective, the range of the performance, and the specific performance characteristics:

Figure 8.1   Basic Set Up of Rubric

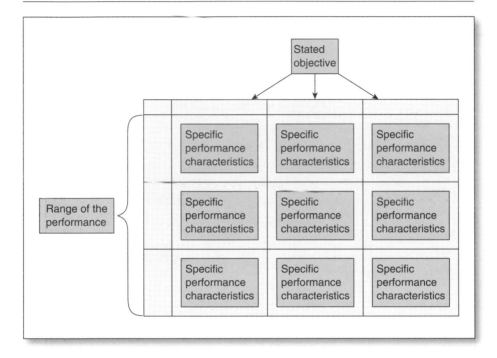

You could certainly have more ranges, more objectives, and more specific performance characteristics, but in the spirit of keeping it simple, keep it at three.

There are six simple steps to creating a rubric:

- Step 1: Decide the range of performance.
- Step 2: Create categories.
- Step 3: Provide descriptors in each category.
- Step 4: Have a tiered system to the descriptors.
- Step 5: Make sure descriptors are specific and not vague.
- Step 6: Check the rubric over.

These steps were first introduced in the book *Performance-Based Assessments for 21st Century Skills* (Stanley, 2014). The first step is to decide the range of performance. As stated before, keep it simple. Give yourself three ranges to consider. You could always have five, one for each letter grade, but three simplifies the process. The more ranges, categories, and descriptors you have, the more complicated using the rubric becomes. If you are evaluating a PBL project that is happening right in front of you, you will need to have the ability to evaluate and assess fairly quickly. Too many categories will slow you down. Two is too few in that you are basically having the student either pass or fail the performance.

Here is a simple rubric with three ranges of performance, using the Invent a Better Mousetrap science project shared in Chapter 7:

Invent a Better Mousetrap

Student: _____

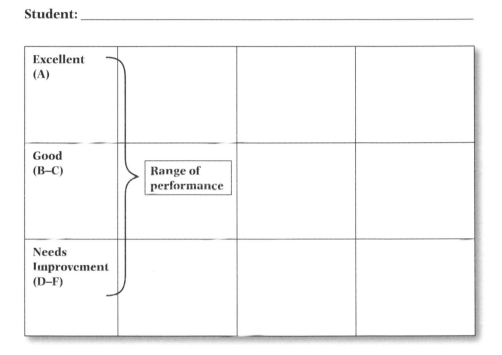

Excellent (A)			
Good (B–C)	Range of performance		
Needs Improvement (D–F)			

The ranges of performance have been divided into excellent, good, and needs improvement. This allows students to see what an excellent project looks like. It also shows them what to avoid unless they want to end up in the good or needs improvement category.

The second step would be to create categories. Things to consider when doing this are the following:

- Decide how many overall categories you want to evaluate.
  - o Usually no fewer than two (not enough to make objective)
  - o No more than four (gets too confusing)
- Decide the weight of each category.

Invent a Better Mousetrap

Student: _____

	Design	Model	Comparison
Excellent (A)			
Good (B–C)			
Needs Improvement (D–F)			

Categories

For this project, the teacher determined the three categories he wanted to focus on: design, model, and comparison. Again, staying with the number three, the teacher has enough categories to break down the overall product, but not so many that it is impossible to keep up. Each can be graded in its own category, and when you add the categories up, you have the entire performance-based assessment. They are basically like pieces of a puzzle. Separately, they show some of the picture, but you have to put them all together in order to see the full product.

Step number three is to provide descriptors for each of the categories chosen.

- Each category should have two to four skills being evaluated.
- This breakdown allows the evaluation to be objective.
- Start at highest range category.

It is best to start at the highest-range category. This way the teacher can envision the ideal project and set a high expectation for students:

Invent a Better Mousetrap

Student: _____

	Design	Model	Comparison
Excellent (A)	• Design clearly takes you step by step how to make it. • Design it clearly labeled with measurements and parts. • Design looks neat and professional.	Descriptors	
Good (B–C)			
Needs Improvement (D–F)			

Again going with the three, three descriptions allows the category to be broken down into enough parts the student can see what needs to be done in order to be successful in the category. For content, students know they will need to focus on three aspects in their design in order to be considered excellent: (1) it clearly takes you step by step how to make it, (2) is clearly labeled with measurements and parts, and (3) looks neat and professional. This is a blueprint for the student. If the student constructs her project following these descriptors, she can guarantee herself an excellent rating for the design.

Once the bar has been set in the excellent range, it simply becomes a matter of showing what it looks like when it is only good or needs improvement. The content of the descriptor is the same, but the level with which the student is achieving is where the change occurs. That is where Step 4 comes into play, creating the tier system for the other ranges in the category.

- Each descriptor should have a matching descriptor at each level. In other words, the skill being assessed should be described on all levels of the range.
- Make sure each level is realistic. Highest range should have high expectations.
- Using *but* for good and *not* for needs improvement.

The simplest way to do this is using the term *but* for the middle range and *not* for the lowest. Here is what the tiered system would look like for our example:

Invent a Better Mousetrap

Student: _____

	Design	Model	Comparison
Excellent (A) tiered	• Design clearly takes you step by step how to make it. • Design it clearly labeled with measurements and parts. • Design looks neat and professional		
Good (B–C) *(but)*	• Design shows you how to make it but skips steps, making it hard to reproduce. • Design is labeled with measurements and parts but missing some in places. • Design looks neat and professional for most part but sloppy in places.		
Needs Improvement (D–F) *(not)*	• Design doesn't really show someone could make it, leaves many steps out. • Design is not labeled with either measurements and or parts. • Design does not look neat and professional; sloppy and hard to see.		

The simple difference between the use of details and examples is the use of a *but* or *not*.

Excellent: Design clearly takes you step by step how to make it.

Good: Design shows you how to make it *but* skips steps, making it hard to reproduce.

Needs Improvement: Design does *not* really show how someone could make it and leaves many steps out.

Keep in mind these descriptors need to be very clear so that students can imagine them. When writing them a teacher must ask himself, "What does this look like?" If a teacher assembled these three descriptors together, the combined result would be either an excellent, good, or product that needs improvement. Sometimes, it is difficult to break down a project into parts like this, but if the teacher cannot do it, how can he expect the students to be able to do the same?

Once the first category is complete, the others just repeat the same process. Keep in mind a couple of things in Step 5:

- You should be able to apply this phrase to each descriptor "What does it look like?"
- Use specific numbers or a range if the category lends itself to it.
- Don't set the bar too high or too low in the wrong evaluation.

Often times, teachers want to use the word *some* in the description of a category such as the following statement: *includes some examples.* The problem with the word some is that it is very vague and is subject to much interpretation. Technically, two dollars is some money, and so is one hundred dollars, but there is a vast difference between those two. Not to mention the student definition of some and the teacher definition might be far apart. A student might define some examples as two, while the teacher might be thinking this means five. Rather than having the student try to guess what the teacher might mean, when applicable, the teacher should use a specific range so that it is clear to the student.

The final step for the rubric would be to check it over and make sure it is going to work. When doing a PBL for the first time, it can be difficult to envision what the final product is going to look like so creating a usable rubric can be a challenge. Here are some tips to ensuring that the rubric will be a successful one:

- Go through each category looking through the tiers to be sure it flows and makes sense.
- Practice grading a performance and see how practical it is (maybe dress rehearsal or another venue).
- Have students or another teacher look it over for any mistakes they might find.

You would take your final rubric which looks something like this and check it over:

Invent a Better Mousetrap

Student: _____

	Design	Model	Comparison
Excellent (A)	• Design clearly takes you step by step how to make it. • Design is clearly labeled with measurements and parts. • Design looks neat and professional.	• Model looks exactly like the design. • Model is durable and built sturdy so it can last. • Model works, trapping the rat without harming it.	• You clearly compare your design with the design of the original mousetrap. • You present both advantages and disadvantages of both traps. • You give good detail and examples why one trap is better than the other.
Good (B-C)	• Design shows you how to make it, but skips steps, making it hard to reproduce. • Design is labeled with measurements and parts, but missing some in places. • Design looks neat and professional for most part, but sloppy in places.	• Model looks pretty much like the design with only a couple of minor changes. • Model is durable and built sturdy, but wouldn't last for very long. • Model works for the most part, trapping the rat without harming it, but having a couple of errors.	• You compare your design with the design of the original mousetrap, but not always able to understand. • You present advantages or disadvantages of the traps but not both. • You explain why one trap is better than the other, but do not include much detail or give examples.
Needs Improvement (D-F)	• Design doesn't really show how someone could make it. It leaves many steps out. • Design is not labeled with either measurements and/or parts. • Design does not look neat and professional; sloppy and hard to see.	• Model looks nothing like the design. • Model is not durable and built sturdy, wouldn't last for more than a couple of uses. • Model does not work or falls apart while trying to trap, or it harms the rat.	• You do not compare your design with the design of the original mousetrap. • You do not present either advantages or disadvantages of both traps. • You do not explain why one trap is better than the other.

Sometimes, you will check it over very thoroughly and be convinced it is going to be a success, only to discover problems that appear when the rubric is being used in the field. It may be an unrealistic range, a skill that is not showing itself in the product, a skill that was overlooked, or something of the type. In that case, evaluate the product with what you have and make the changes the next go around. It would not be fair to hold students accountable for something that was not included in the rubric you gave them ahead of time.

CREATING RUBRICS WITH STUDENTS

One way to have students even more invested in a rubric and truly understand what it is evaluating is to create the rubric together as a class. When a teacher gives a rubric to students at the beginning of the project, students might glance at it or maybe even leave it behind when the bell rings. By creating the rubric as a class, it makes the students more aware of what is in it because they contributed to its content.

In order to do this you would follow the same six steps used when creating your own rubric only the students would help to create the range, categories, and descriptors. Having students come up with the categories allows them to break down the product into parts so they can see for themselves the components that make a successful PBL. This especially helps those students who have trouble seeing the big picture. The dialogue of the class debate on what it a valid descriptor and what is not is also very enlightening because students become very clear on what would be acceptable and what would not.

Even though you as the teacher are leading the discussion, allowing students to arrive at conclusions for themselves and deciding what makes for different levels of range can be very powerful. Plus there is the empowerment of determining for themselves how they are going to be assessed. Most times, students have no say in this matter, but here you are allowing them their input. In most cases, they will arrive at the same decisions you would have made yourself but in this scenario they feel as though they were made part of the process. This allows them to connect to the evaluation process and have a better understanding of how the product is evaluated. The skill of making a really good, objective rubric is something that can be taught to learners of all ages. If you give students choice when working on a project, they may need a rubric that is tailor-made to their final product. In this case, the students should create a rubric that fits the needs of their particular product.

PERFORMANCE REVIEWS (SELF/PEER EVALUATIONS)

Many times in a PBL, the rubric only evaluates the end product. The problem with this is if the project has been going on for 2, 3, even 4 weeks, that is a lot of ground to cover with a single evaluation. You need to have a way to evaluate the process of PBL. One way is by using a performance review. Just as in a business, a performance review is an evaluation of a job performance. In this case, the job is the project that students are working on. Assessments should be done intermittently throughout the project, chronicling different aspects of the work. This allows students to not only be evaluated on the product, but also the process which is one of the most important aspects of PBL. This also gives them a chance to make up for mistakes and to maintain focus over the course of many weeks. Think of it like having several snapshots of the students as they progress through the project. By putting these snapshots together, you get a clear picture of the student's efforts.

A performance assessment needs to be broken down just as the project itself is broken down. Here is an example that can be found in the Reproducibles section of the book as well:

	Self:	Peer:	Peer:
Research			
Creation of Product			
Lesson Preparation/ Presentation			

The project requires three parts. There is the initial research where students are using books or the Internet to gather information needed for the content of their product. The second part is the actual making of the product: what physically needs to be done and what materials will be necessary to do it. The final part of the project involves creating the lesson the students will use to teach the class. This involves planning and practicing the lesson before giving it (part of the design review process). What you are asking a student to do is to evaluate the effort of himself or herself and his or her peers during each of these parts. The student is not evaluating the quality of the product; that is for the teacher to determine in the rubric. Instead he will be determining whether the peer did what she was supposed to as well as how effective a group member she was. If you have created norms as a class, these can be used to determine how effective the group member was. The student performance review determines how well the student lived up to the norms the group established.

Just as mentioned earlier in the chapter, have students keep it simple. Use a rating system that they are already familiar with such as on a scale from 1 to 10 or an excellent, good, and needs improvement to mimic the categories in the project rubric. One that students are all too familiar with that can be used are letter grades. You as the teacher just need to be clear what each of those letters indicate about the student's effort:

- A = excellent
- B = good
- C = average
- D = poor
- F = failure

This might involve having a conversation about what each of these looks like and having a high expectation of an A rather than giving someone an A because they did what they were supposed to. In addition to putting a grade, students must justify the reason for the evaluation they gave with a sentence or two explanation. These performance reviews will be filled out over the course of a project at the direction of the teacher resulting in three to six snapshots of student effort. The final results might look like this:

	Self: *Nicolas*	**Peer:** *James*	**Peer:** *Nathan*
Research	B) *Worked well, lots of research, stayed on task* B) *Worked great, got same research done, stayed on task well*	A) *Outstanding work, always working, good research, helped us all stay on task* B) *Worked well, got lots of research, stayed on task*	D) *Did not do much work or research and got off task* B) *Great improvement worked hard and well, researched lots stayed on task*
Creation of Product	B) *Stayed on task, lots of research, helped tons with model and act*	B) *Very helpful, got some research done, helped a lot with act and model; stayed on task*	B) *On task most of the time, helped a ton with model and act, great ideas, did some research*
Lesson Preparation/ Presentation	B) *Stayed on task, helped with both models but not as much*	B) *Stayed on task, helped a lot with model (armor)*	B) *Stayed on task, helped tons with model (weapon) and act*

There can be issues when students are evaluating themselves and others. Some of these in business according to Dartmouth College are

- Halo Effect: The tendency to make inappropriate generalizations from one aspect of a person's job performance. This is due to being influenced by one or more outstanding characteristics, either positive or negative.
- Leniency: The tendency to evaluate all people as outstanding and to give inflated ratings rather than true assessments of performance.
- Central Tendency: The tendency to evaluate every person as average regardless of differences in performance.
- Strictness: The tendency to rate all people at the low end of the scale and are overly critical of performance.
- Contrast Effect: The tendency for a rater to evaluate a person relative to other individuals rather than on-the-job requirements.
- First Impression Error: The tendency for a manager to make an initial favorable or unfavorable judgment about someone, and then ignore subsequent information that does not support this impression.
- Similar-to-Me Effect: The tendency to more favorably judge those people perceived as similar to the leader (Human).

These are the same things that affect student peer and self-evaluations. Like most things with PBL and managing your classroom, with proper training many of these issues can resolved. Holding a workshop where you show students objective ways to evaluate peers and going over exemplary examples will help students to understand what these should look like and what the teacher is expecting. For instance, the teacher could provide examples of acceptable grades for each of the levels and their justifications:

- A: She worked hard the entire time, producing four pages of notes that she shared with the group.
- B: He spent most of the class researching causes of photosynthesis, but there were a couple of times I saw him on sites that had nothing to do with our topic.
- C: She was goofing off from time to time, talking with friends not even in our group.
- D: Although there were times he was on task, making suggestions to the group about the final product, most times he was not on-task

and got other people off-task as well by talking to them about things other than the project

- F: He was working on his math homework the entire time while the rest of us did research.

There should also be discussions about justifications that are not acceptable. This again would involve providing examples of what this looks like:

- A: Great job (too general with no evidence)
- B: She spent most of the time talking to a friend but did manage to do a little research (description does not seem to match a B grade).
- C: He worked really hard, finding lots of good information about photosynthesis and even a great video that he shared with everyone (seems to be grading too hard).
- D: Off-task like 90% of the time (needs examples).
- F: This person was mean to me (more about personal issues rather than the efforts of the student).

What performance reviews do is make students accountable for their work in a collaborative learning setting. Students are going to be evaluated by the members of their groups, so they must make sure to live up to the group norms. If they do not, there is a chance the group members will evaluate them in an unfavorable way. This makes it easier on the teacher because rather than one set of eyes looking for students who are not doing what they are supposed to be, there are now an entire classroom of eyes. Performance reviews also make the student beholden to his peers for his grade rather than it being the sole responsibility of the teacher.

When students finish the project, they should turn in their performance reviews. If the group had five group members, you take the four peer evaluations and one self and average them into a single grade, keeping the performance reviews as documentation. You as the teacher also give input into the performance review grades. If you viewed the student off-task more than her group admitted, and they are just covering for her, you can change the grade to reflect this, making sure to tell the student that you made this decision. The teacher can also play the tiebreaker. If the average grade from the performance reviews is bordering between a B– and a C+, the teacher can determine which way it is going to go based on his own observations of the student throughout the project. By conducting the performance reviews in this manner you get 360 degree feedback, which means the student receives multiple evaluations including the teacher, fellow students, and himself. These evaluations individually might have bias and subjectivity, but combined together, they form an objective evaluation of the student performance.

At Least Manage This

According to H. Goodrich (1996), in order to use rubrics effectively in the classroom you must have the following criteria:

1. Have students look at models of good versus "not-so-good" work. A teacher could provide sample assignments of variable quality for students to review.

2. List the criteria to be used in the scoring rubric and allow for discussion of what counts as quality work. Asking for student feedback during the creation of the list also allows the teacher to assess the students' overall writing experiences.

3. Articulate gradations of quality. These hierarchical categories should concisely describe the levels of quality (ranging from bad to good) or development (ranging from beginning to mastery). They can be based on the discussion of the good versus not-so-good work samples or immature versus developed samples. Using a conservative number of gradations keeps the scoring rubric user-friendly while allowing for fluctuations that exist within the average range.

4. Practice on models. Students can test the scoring rubrics on sample assignments provided by the instructor. This practice can build students' confidence by teaching them how the instructor would use the scoring rubric on their papers. It can also aid student/teacher agreement on the reliability of the scoring rubric.

5. Ask for self and peer-assessment.

6. Revise the work on the basis of that feedback. As students are working on their assignment, they can be stopped occasionally to do a self-assessment and then give and receive evaluations from their peers. Revisions should be based on the feedback they receive.

7. Use teacher assessment, which means using the same scoring rubric the students used to assess their work (pp. 15–16).

Based on the criteria laid out in this list, it would be safe to assume that if you were to follow the steps laid out for you in this chapter, you will be able to create rubrics that evaluate PBL in your classroom in an objective manner by making them both valid and reliable.

Managing the Classroom

Of all the things I've done, the most vital is coordinating the talents of those who work for us and pointing them towards a certain goal.

—Walt Disney

You have created the project, you have introduced it to the students, and you have given them a syllabus and rubric to guide them. Now as the teacher, what do you do? Just like project managers in the business world, you inspire your people to produce the highest quality product possible by coordinating their talents and pointing them to a specific goal. Like most things with project-based learning (PBL), this is much easier said than done. What does this inspiration look like? What strategies work best with students? How does the role of the teacher in a PBL classroom differ from the role of a teacher in a traditional classroom?

ORIENTATION/TRAINING YOUR STUDENTS

When an employee starts a new job, usually the first thing he must experience is an orientation. This might involve listening to someone explain the philosophies of the organization, filling out paperwork, watching videos designed to train you in certain aspects, and basically getting an overview for what the job will entail. Although it can seem tedious, it is necessary to provide one with the background information he will need in order to do his job. How will you know how to access files unless it is shown to you? How will you know if you are following company protocol unless someone makes you aware of it? How will you even know where to store your lunch unless someone shows you where the refrigerator is? To start workers out on the correct foot, businesses orient them to the basics of how the company/office works. *Forbes Magazine* states the importance of this orientation: "The first few minutes of new employee orientation, if done right, can lead to happier and more productive workers and, ultimately, increased customer satisfaction" (Noble, 2013, Paragraph 2).

This is why it is important to have your own orientation for students. This will set the tone for the class and help them to understand their role. Because you might be asking students to learn in a way they are not familiar with, they might be uncomfortable with some of the methods of PBL. In order to familiarize and get them comfortable with the process, a good employee orientation will go a long way in setting the proper environment for the classroom. It will make for happier and more productive students.

According to *BC Jobs,* there are five things that make for a successful employee orientation (Alud, 2010):

Tip #1: Needs to answer the following questions:

- What is this organization really about?
- What is it like to work here?
- How are things organized?
- Where do I find what I need to do my job?
- And . . . where does my job fit in?

Tip #2: Needs to be memorable

Tip #3: Help them build their social network

Tip #4: Think of orientation as a process, not an event. Orientation is not a one-time event.

Tip #5: Many businesses don't really provide an orientation program, and this is probably the biggest mistake they can make. Even if you don't have an "official" program—you do indeed have an orientation. Consider the following: The employee forms his or her own opinion of the company based on those he or she meets upon arrival (Auld, 2010).

This chapter will address all of these tips and how to properly set up an orientation in your own PBL classroom.

LAYING THE GROUNDWORK

What should your classroom orientation look like? Different teachers do it in different ways. Some go over the classroom rules with the students. Others go step-by-step through classroom procedures. Some teachers might have an icebreaker or some other activity designed to allow the students to have fun while learning about one another and what they did over the summer. For the project manager classroom, you will want to establish the philosophy that students have choice in their education. This might seem foreign to some students who are used to having the teacher tell them what to do all the time and directing their work in a prescribed manner. The PBL classroom is rife with choices; choices on topics, products, partners, methods of research, sources, etc. This is why the orientation should reflect these choices and philosophy of teaching.

A good activity to set this tone is Decisions Decisions or some similar activity that provides choice. Decisions Decisions is a computer simulation that comes complete with advisor handbooks and a teacher workbook. They have various editions, from the environment, forming a constitution, immigration, revolutionary war, ancient empires, prejudice, on the campaign trail, and feudalism. In Decisions Decisions, students are broken into groups. In these groups, every student plays a specific role. For example, in the Decisions Decisions for ancient empires, there are four advisors; the trader's daughter, the warrior, the elder, and the poet. Students are presented with a dilemma for which they must try and figure out a solution. In the ancient empires, an invader by the name of Lozar is said to be heading toward your city-state, and the people must figure out what they are going to do. Students first read about and get background information pertaining to the dilemma. This provides them with the context of the situation and to understand their roles a bit better. Then the group must set a goal. There are four goals provided, and they must rank them in importance using the information they have just read. In the ancient empires simulation, the four goals are

A. Preserve Tyber's culture and way of life
B. Maintain power
C. Please the goddess Elyra
D. Ensure the well-being of Tyber's people

Students in their groups must discuss, debate, and decide how to prioritize these goals. Which one is the most important one? Which one is of lesser concern? Once the goals are ranked, students are reminded that every choice they make from here on out needs to take them toward the top goal and they should avoid choices that would take them away. Then students will have to make five decisions presented one at a time. Each decision leads to certain consequences, which can be good or bad, and additional choices. For each decision, each advisor is given a different key word. Students read a paragraph or so of information and then share this with their group. Then the group must take all the information that has been shared and make the best possible decision that will allow them to accomplish the goal they prioritized. After the five decisions are made students find out the fate of their dilemma, and they reflect how well they succeeded in reaching their goals.

Decisions Decisions sets the expectations for a few areas in the classroom:

- Collaboration
- Information literacy
- Importance of setting goals
- Making informed choices
- Performance aspect
- Reflection

These are all skills the students will be employing for the entire year in the classroom, so modeling it in their first activity sets the tone and orients them on the expectations of the class.

You do not have to use Decisions Decisions specifically, but you should find an orientation activity that allows students to have choice and that sets the classroom environment and expectations. Laying this groundwork is so important to getting the most from students using PBL.

MAKING THE STRUCTURE CLEAR

The project management classroom needs to have a structure to it. Although students might have different choices to make throughout the year and the products might change, the basic structure of the classroom will remain the same. Whether students are learning about Ancient China or chemical changes or literary analogies, students will be following the same basic steps for projects:

1. Setting a goal

2. Creating a plan

3. Gathering information needed to fulfill the plan

4. Learn basic skills to make the product

5. Creating the product

6. Reflecting on what was learned

The elements within this structure might change depending on whether you use a contract, calendar, or a rubric, but the basic structure will pretty much remain the same. Making sure your students are familiar with this structure and are comfortable to learn within it is important, which is why you want to train students to make sure they understand.

In your orientation training, you will want to expose students to this structure. Hopefully, your opening activity has modeled this basic structure, but you will want to put it into the context of a lesson so that students can see it in action. Go over what the expectations would be for each of these parts of the structure, so students know how they are expected to act. It might look something like this (PowerPoint Presentation containing these bullet points can be found on the website http://rcsources.corwin.com/StanleyCreatingLearners):

Setting a Goal

- Think about what you want to accomplish in this project:
  o Can be specific such as a certain grade you want to attain
  o Can be more general such as completing it on time

- Goal needs to be realistically attainable:
  o Do not bite off more than you can chew
  o Do not set unachievable goals

- Need to revisit goal periodically throughout the project
  o Each time you make a decision you need to consider your goal
  o Is your decision taking you toward your goal or away from it?

Creating a Plan

- What are your learning outcomes for the project?
  o In other words, what would someone learn from looking at your product?

- What skills will be necessary to complete this project?
  o Do you have these skills or will you have to learn them?

- What product will best demonstrate what it is you wish to show?
  o Fitting the proper product with the proper project

Gathering Information Needed to Fulfill the Plan

- How will you get the information you need to complete your product?
  - o Internet research
  - o Books
  - o Interviews

- How will you plan to cite the sources of where you got this information?
  - o Using MLA format or something of the like to cite sources
  - o Getting used to writing down websites and sources when conducting research

- How will you synthesize the information you gather in order to avoid plagiarizing?
  - o How to put it into your own words effectively

Learn Basic Skills to Make the Product

- Does your product/project require you to learn a skill in order to complete the product?
  - o PowerPoint, podcast, video conference, movie maker, etc.

- How will you acquire these skills?
  - o Will the teacher provide some guidance?
  - o Do you need to learn it on your own?
  - o Is there an expert that can be used as a resource?

- At what point do you need to know these skills?
  - o Cannot wait until too long because it might prevent you from reaching your deadline
  - o If there are several skills that need to be learned, in what order should you learn them (prioritize)?

Creating the Product

- If you have a choice in the product, does the product you have chosen properly convey the information it needs to?
  - o Rule of thumb: Could someone learn from looking at your product?

- How much time will be needed to create the product?
  - o Time management skills come into play

- How will you deliver the product?
    - Do you have to make a physical product?
    - Is it a presentation that needs to be scheduled/arranged?
    - Will you be needing assistance in getting the product in?

Reflection

- What did you learn from this project/activity?
    - Could be about the content, time management, self-awareness, etc.
- What mistakes did you make that could be avoided next time?
    - They are not mistakes if you learn from them. If you keep repeating them however you will get the same results.
- How did you feel about the project/activity?
    - This allows students to explore their feelings and thoughts
    - Allows for self-reflection

Make sure students are as familiar with this structure as possible because it will be the process they use for the entire school year. If you have the advantage of having the same students over the course of a couple of years, it is even better because then they come in the next year properly trained.

MODEL THE STRUCTURE WITH A MINI-PROJECT

To acquaint students with the structure, a good strategy is to conduct a mini-project to demonstrate how it works. This should not be a long-term project but rather a couple of days at the most, which gives the teacher enough time to run through all aspects of the structure, but brief enough for students to get the point. Choosing a topic that students already have some knowledge about or would care about in addition to having plenty of easily accessible research works best. If you try and introduce something the students know nothing about, it bogs down the process, which is not the point of this activity. The point of this activity is for students to learn the skill of working on a project, not the content. Some examples of good topics would be:

- Are requiring school uniforms a good thing for schools?
- Should students be able to bring their cell phones to school?
- Is age 16 a good age for people to be able to drive on the road?

- If you download music/movies that you did not pay for is that the same as stealing?
- Which season is the best (fall, winter, spring, summer)?
- Does attending school year-round benefit students?
- Who is better, Jordan or Lebron?

An example that could be used in the classroom is the paper vs. plastic mini-project. This is a 2-day project where students must determine which is better; paper or plastic, when asking for bags at the grocery store. Students will need to justify their decision using research. Then students must present their decision and evidence to the class in some sort of product. The mini-project should go in the same order the structure you wish to use throughout the year will follow. The one we have used in this chapter is this:

Step #1: Setting a goal

Step #2: Creating a plan

Step #3: Gathering information needed to fulfill the plan

Step #4: Learn basic skills to make the product

Step #5: Creating the product

Step #6: Reflecting on the process

As with any project, you need to provide deadlines for students to follow. This enables them to manage their time better and not spend too much effort on one thing and not enough on another. Here is a basic timeline for the paper vs. plastic mini-project (can be adjusted to fit your schedule and length of periods):

- 1 minute to set a goal
- 5 minutes to develop a plan/roles
- 35 minutes to research (inquiry, exploration)
- 30 minutes to learn how and create a product
- 3 minutes each to present
- 5 minutes to reflect on the process

Your job as the project manager is to remind students of these deadlines. Keep them apprised on how much time they have left for a particular activity. A long-term project would involve looking at the calendar and giving them suggestions where they should be in the project at any given time. In a mini-project such as this, it means playing time keeper where you are updating them every 5 to 10 minutes so that they do not get caught up in their work and not leave enough time to complete it. This will be a good lesson on time management as some students will not be able to find all of the research they need or to finish their product. Because this mini-project is not graded though this is alright and part of the process of learning from mistakes.

Because students will be working in groups often for their projects, this example should be no different. Figure out a way to divide the class into groups of three or four students. One easy way since it is the beginning of the year is simply to do it alphabetically, going every three people on your class roster. You can have students count off, draw popsicle sticks, pick their own groups, or whatever.

The first step in their groups will be setting a goal. Because this is a mini-project, only give them a minute to set their goal. This will be a good exercise in goal setting because there is no grade attached, which is usually the goal of most schoolwork for students. Instead they will have to set a goal based on the limited structure such as managing time well, working well together, or something to do with the process of the project rather than the final product. Have groups go around and announce their goals so the other students hear different possibilities for goals. You as the teacher may need to help them turn the goal into a good one because either they are too specific or not specific enough. Have each group write their goal somewhere where it is visible throughout the mini-project.

Once the goal had been set, the next step is to create a plan. Because this is a mini-project, students do not have the luxury of taking a lot of time to create their plan. To help them out, provide the learning objectives for them:

Paper versus Plastic

- What are the advantages or disadvantages of using paper for your grocery bag?
- What are the advantages or disadvantages of using plastic for your grocery bag?
- Which of the two do you think would be best to use and why?
- Is there are third alternative that would be better than paper or plastic?

These learning objectives guide the students in their research and creation of the product just as it will when they create their own learning objectives. These learning outcomes are fairly open-ended, allowing students a lot of breadth when deciding how to approach the project. It is also a common topic with a lot of information out there. By providing the learning outcomes students can focus their planning more so on what the product is going to be and what roles each member is going to play in the group as well as speeds up the process.

Students need to figure out which side they are going to take in this debate. Do students see paper as being a better option or does plastic seem like a better choice? Students can plan to make this decision at the very beginning so the research they look for is supporting their position, or they can choose to hold off on this decision until they have done some research and then arrive at it. Either way, groups will need to decide how they are going to proceed on the project together so that everyone is working toward the same purpose. It is when members of a group are unsure of what direction the group is moving in that confusion begins to settle in and causes all sorts of issues.

Students would need to plan what sort of product they are going to create in order to guide them in their project. For instance, if the group decides to do a PowerPoint, they would need to figure out if someone knows how to do this. Or if the group wants to make a puppet show, do they have the necessary materials and time to create them. Often times with a product students can choose something they think is creative and fun, but ends up being impractical. Students need to weigh what is the best product that will enable its listener/viewer to gain an understanding of what the group is trying to demonstrate. Groups could certainly wait until they have their research to decide on a product, but by having it chosen ahead of time, the research becomes more purposeful. In other words, if the group is going to make a visual poster, noting where good images or charts/graphs are from the research will help in the creation of the product. Or if students have decided to stage a mock interview, noting the names of experts from this research whose roles they can play in the interview would be helpful.

Notice in both of these aspects, the product and the side of the argument, students have the choice to make a decision at the beginning or later on in the project. The group needs to make sure this is the group plan. If the plan is to wait until the research is collected until making a decision which one to support, or the plan from the very beginning is to do a talk show for the presentation as the product, the group needs to agree on this approach. You do not want half of the group assuming they are arguing one side only to discover the group is choosing the other. By making this a part of their plan, everyone is on the same page and working toward the same goal.

Now that students have a clear goal and have developed a plan, they will need to gather information. The teacher/project manager needs to be sure to provide resources for this whether this means having a library of books on the topic, printing off articles for the students to read, or providing laptops/computers to conduct Internet research. Throughout this process, you as the project manager should be reminding students of the time and when they need to get started on the next part of the project. As they begin to work on the product, the group will need to determine is there some skill they need to learn in order to create it. If the group decided to do a Prezi, does someone in the group already have an account or do enough people in the group know how to create a Prezi to get a product done in the limited time they have been given. Or if the students are writing a script and using Google Docs to write it together, might someone in the group need to learn how to use Google Docs and how to access their account? In a long-term project the students would have more time to learn how to create a particular product. If they are doing a podcast, they might spend a class looking at how they are made and various formats they can take. In a quick project such as this though, they need to choose a product they can create quickly given the allotted time. As the project manager, this is where you will need to make sure students have not bitten off more than can chew. You do not want to discourage students from creating an ambitious product but at the same time, you might need to remind them of the realities of the product and help them to determine whether it is indeed the best one for the project.

When the students have finished their product, they must give their 3-minute presentation. Three minutes does not sound like much time, but you would be surprised how many students do not fill the allotted time. The 3-minute limit also focuses students on the main arguments of their topic and prevents them from rambling on about things that are not as important. It is a time management exercise to see if they can get what they need to say in the time they have as well as developing it enough for an audience to understand their argument. If you do not provide time limits, you could end up with long-winded products that bore students rather than teach them.

As the project manager, you should provide feedback to students on the spot after each presentation. This is not designed to embarrass any students nor should the teacher set out to do this, but pointing out things that worked well and things that did not can be a learning experience for that group as well as the other students. You can even involve the audience, asking them to give one positive feedback and one room for improvement. This way students are seeing successful examples they can model later as well as seeing mistakes they will hopefully avoid.

With the products presented you need to make sure to provide time for students to reflect upon the activity. Using a protocol to run a reflection is usually a good idea rather than just telling them to reflect. For instance, you might have them journal privately what they thought worked well and did not and then have them share their thoughts with the group. One protocol that is simple yet effective is the What/So What/Now What. It looks like this:

What:

- Descriptive
- Facts, what happened, with whom
- Substance of group interaction

So What:

- Shift from descriptive to interpretive
- Meaning of experience for each participant
- Feelings involved, lessons learned
- Why?

Now What:

- Contextual—seeing this situation's place in the big picture
- Applying lessons learned/insights gained to new situations
- Setting future goals, creating an action plan

Give students 5 minutes at the end of the mini-project to use a protocol such as this to guide their reflection. Students might learn more from this than they do from the actual project.

WHAT TRAINING WILL BE IMPORTANT TO THE JOB?

Now that students are aware of the structure and you have modeled this for them in the mini-project, as the teacher you will need to determine if there is any additional training students will need in order to successfully work on projects in your classroom. For instance, if you determine that students will be doing a lot of Internet research, it might be a good idea to hold a workshop on how to do this well. Or if your science class is going to be using a fab lab often, getting the students into the lab at the very beginning and training them the proper way to use it will go a long way in making future projects that much more smooth. Maybe you will be using a computer program like geometer sketchpad for students to be able to create 3-dimensional geometry patterns and so giving a brief tutorial on that would be beneficial for future projects involving that program.

This process requires there to be a lot of forethought into the course of the school year. In other words, if you are the type of teacher who does not know what they will be teaching from week to week because you are creating lesson plans on the go, this makes it difficult to anticipate what skills students are going to need. If, however, you have a general idea of what is going to be taught and what product will be attached to it, it allows you to determine what training needs to take place. The planning need not be detailed and extensive. It can be something general such as the following:

	6th Grade	**Product**
First 6 Weeks	Mesopotamia/China/India	Podcast
Second 6 Weeks	Egypt	Museum exhibit
Third 6 Weeks	Africa	Multicultural fair
Fourth 6 Weeks	Model United Nations—Africa	Oral defense of resolution
Fifth 6 Weeks	Geography—World Religions	PowerPoint presentation/Interview
Sixth 6 Weeks	Economics—Shark Tank	Business plan

This teacher may not have figured out exactly how each unit is going to unfold, but he has a general idea and knows that oral presentation is going to factor into many of the products and so might want to conduct a training to prepare students. Other skills such as the PowerPoints, podcasts, a business plan, and a museum exhibit are specific to only a single project so the teacher might want to wait until students are working on that particular project before training them.

PROVIDING MENTAL SPACE

When we think of the classroom, we often associate it with a physical space. How are the desks arranged, is there adequate room for students to meet as a group, is the technology in the classroom up-to-date? More important than this physical space is the mental space. What this means for the project manager is finding a spot where you know what is going on with all projects, but you may not know what is going on at all times. Just like employees in an office, if students feel you are micromanaging their project, they will not have the freedom to be creative and try things in the risk zone of learning. Not only that, if you micromanage the project too much, it will turn out exactly like you would have created the project. That is not what you want from students, a cookie cutter assembly line of products. You want students to bring their creativity, experiences, and ideas to the product. You want to be able to communicate with groups and help them when they need it. You also want to give them space to make mistakes they can learn from and allow them to learn adaptability, a 21st century survival skill. You need to motivate students in their work by commending what they have already done and encouraging them to take risks and reach deeper levels of learning. You want to be there to problem solve if necessary but usually only in a last resort situation. You should allow groups to work out their own problems using the norms, but let them know you have their backs and are paying attention to what is going on. The balance of this looks something like Figure 9.1 (Richman, 2012, p. 148):

Figure 9.1

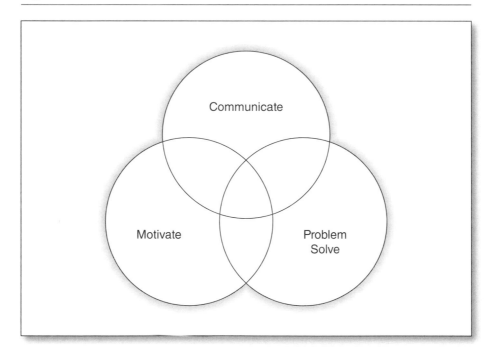

Notice one aspect does not dominate the other, rather there is a balance. And there is plenty of space in this configuration to allow students to create and take risks. The trick as the project manager is finding this balance. Much of this can be established through the three steps of managing others: 1) observe, 2) react, and 3) evaluate (Richman, 2012, p. 153). During the *observe* aspect, from a distance look for signs that students are struggling or are dealing with conflict. If they are, observe how they are handling it. It is only when they have tried to solve the problem and have exhausted all of their own methods that the teacher should *react* and intervene. When you do have to react you should not just be giving them the answer to their problem. You should guide groups to solve the problem on their own. Help them to come to a solution that acts as a compromise for all parties involved. *Evaluate* comes in the verbal teacher feedback you provide for how students are working in groups and how they can become more effective in this. It can come in gentle nudges and comments or it can involve an entire conversation or a formal evaluation.

PROJECT MANAGER VERSUS TEACHER

There are four stages to a team's development. They are

1. Forming

2. Storming

3. Norming

4. Performing (Heagney, 2012, p. 162)

Forming is when the group first gets together and is trying to figure out what the project will look like. Much of the forming stage will be creating the contract for the project and setting team goals. During this time, students will also determine what their specific roles are going to be so they know their place in the group.

The storming stage is when a group hits a speed bump or runs into a wall. If you have set up solid norms and are employing the use of performance reviews where students evaluate one another, much of this takes care of itself. You must give students the chance to run into these obstacles and then see how they handle adapting to them. This is part of the process of learning how to collaborate and becoming more adaptable. If it does seem a group cannot navigate around the problem, you as the project manager may have to react to this to be make sure the storming does not spiral out of control and ruin the project.

The third stage is the norming. This is where groups are getting down to brass tacks and actually getting the work done. Because you have established class norms and the group has set a goal for themselves, hopefully groups will achieve this stage fairly quickly so that they can focus most of their attention on the project.

The final stage is performing. This is when the team becomes a well-oiled machine that needs very little direction from the teacher and are motivating one another. Ideally this is where you would like most groups to be. During the performing stage you will utilize the integration process where project managers are coordinating the efforts of the workers toward the accomplishment of the group goal (Pennypacker, 1997, p. 73). This involves keeping students' eyes on the goal and helping them to determine whether actions they are taking for the project are taking them toward or away from it. If it is taking them away, the project manager should help students to adjust their actions so that the project will be successful. Strategies for this would be referring students to their contract, making sure they are following the rubric and the requirements they will be evaluated on, and asking them how the work is coming in the status and process reviews. By getting groups to this stage you have come from being a teacher that directs every aspect of the classroom to a project manager who allows students to learn for themselves through experience and collaboration with peers. The transformation will have been complete.

Each of these stages requires a different style of leading as the teacher/ project manager. In the forming stage, you are using a more directive style of leadership, guiding students through the contract and forming of a group goal, directing much of what they are doing. During the storming phase, the teacher should use influence or persuasion to help students work through their problems. This is more subtle than the directive that is simply telling them how it needs to be done. Instead, it involves taking on a mediator role of helping them to work out their differences or overcoming the obstacle without you telling them exactly how to do this. During the norming stage you should take on a more participatory role and share in the decision making process rather than directing it. This participative role shows itself in the status and process reviews you have with students. In the performing stage, your role becomes a delegative style of leadership where the teacher can just sit back and watch the magic. This is the most rewarding aspect of the project manager model, watching as students take pride in their work and seem to enjoy working with one another to accomplish their goal (Heagney, 2012, pp. 163–165).

CLOSING THE PROJECT

Your final task as project manager is to close the project. This usually is broken down into two parts:

1) Evaluation of the performance in the project

2) Lessons learned/reflection

The evaluation of the performance comes from several perspectives. One perspective is that of the teacher. The grades or evaluations are given back and reflected upon. This involves another stage of conferencing. The teacher and the individual student or group sit down together and have a discussion about the performance. This can typically begin with the teacher asking the students "If you were me, what grade would you have given the performance/product?" Students are usually pretty honest with their grade or are even harder on themselves because they were aware of shortcomings and flaws that might not have made themselves apparent in the final product. Then the teacher would reveal the grade in the form of the rubric and there would be a discussion about whether the assessment of the product was on the same page and where there might have been differences. As the teacher does this he goes over the rubric with the students step by step to make sure they understand how things were evaluated and what could be done for improvement. This allows the students to get a sense for what the teacher is looking for in future projects as well as having successes reinforced that can be used in future projects. The teacher should not just hand back the rubric and allow the students to decipher what they got for themselves. There should be a dialogue to ensure that students are learning from their mistakes and improving for next time.

Another perspective are the group peers of the student. Students should see how their peers evaluated them in the performance reviews, looking over comments for how improvements could be made as well as mistakes. Again, if students are not aware of these deficiencies, how can they possibly avoid that mistake in the future and become a better group member? You could do this in a variety of ways. You could put the groups together and let them discuss the evaluations that were given and the reasoning for it. If this might be too volatile a situation, you can have a class discussion where general reflections upon student effort during the project are made. You would not point out any students in particular but instead would make general references to common patterns amongst the performance reviews. You might do a comparison chart where you show students how they stacked up to other students working on the project.

Do not use the students' names; rather assign them a number, but show everyone's ratings so that they can be compared to their peers. These results are not displayed to embarrass students but to allow them to see where they fall in regard to other students in the classroom. It provides them with a context on how their effort stacks up to others.

1	Fractions Project
2	B+
3	A−
4	B−
5	A
6	A
7	B+
8	A
9	B+
10	A
11	B+
12	C

It is also very powerful to track students' performance reviews over the course of the year. Some students need help with self-awareness. Even when group after group gives them low marks these students tend to blame their group mates for not liking them and do not take any personal responsibility. To help them to see the big picture show them a running tally of student scores in group work:

	Project #1	Project #2	Project #3	Project #4	Project #5
2	B+	A–	A–	A–	A–
3	A–	B+	B	B	B
4	B–	A–	B	B+	A–
5	A	A	A	A	A
6	A	A–	A–	A	A–
7	B+	B–	C	C	C+
8	A	A	A–	A-	A–
9	B+	A–	A	A-	A
10	A	A	A–	A	A
11	B+	A–	A	B+	B+
12	C	B+	A	A–	B–

What you are looking for are patterns. For example, Student #6 seems like a valuable group mate to have, earning high marks consistently. Student #7 seems to have started the year well but has faded on the past few projects. You see a steady progression of improvement in Student #4. Having conversations about patterns will help students to see the larger picture and be able to self-reflect better on their evaluations.

The final perspective is that of the student himself. Only the student can determine what was truly learned from the project. This takes us into the lessons learned part of the closing. What should be built into the timeline of the project is a day or two afterwards to reflect upon the process and what was learned from the project. Some would argue the product is what was learned, but it is important for students to figure out for themselves what was learned. A student might have learned that she is not good at time management. Or that she is very skilled at creating PowerPoints. Or some other skill not tied into the learning objectives but are important nonetheless. This is where students see the 21st skills acquired through the project and the value in them. Some ways to conduct this reflection would be through writing, taking a questionnaire, or just having a conversation. A written reflection would involve a prompt for students to write about. Possible prompts for reflection would be:

- What is something we did during this project that you think you will remember for the rest of your life?
- What was the most challenging part of this project for you?
- What are three things you did during this project to help your classmates?
- What is something that was hard for you at the start of the project, but is easy now?
- In what area do you feel you made your biggest improvements?
- What in our class has made the biggest impact on your learning during this project? Why?
- What is something the teacher could have done to make this project better?
- If you could turn back time and do this project again, what would you do differently?
- What is something you accomplished during this project that you are proud of?
- What was the nicest thing someone in our class did for you during this project?
- If you could change one thing that happened during this project, what would it be?
- What are the three most important things you learned during this project?
- What is something you taught your teacher or classmates during this project?
- What was the best piece of writing that you did during this project? Why do you think it is your best?
- What are six adjectives that best describe this project?
- When you consider the rest of your life, what percentage of what you learned during this project do you think will be useful to you?
- What advice would you give students who will participate in this project next year? (Hewes, 2012)

Students would write on these in a timed session and turn them into the teacher, place them into a student portfolio, or use them as a jump-off point into a class discussion.

A questionnaire reflection might look something like this:

- Project objectives and critical success factors
- Project plan and schedule

- Project team
- Use of technology
- Project monitoring
- Project communications

Students would rate each of these categories based on the following scale:

0 = Don't Know or Not Applicable

Scale from: 1 = Strongly Disagree to 5 = Strongly Agree (Mastering Project Management, 2012, Paragraph 8–9)

You would tabulate the totals and show them to the class to demonstrate the overall learning.

No matter what method you choose, it is very important for the class to reflect upon a project before moving onto the next. Otherwise valuable lessons might be lost or mistakes might continue.

At Least Manage This

The role of the teacher in a PBL is much different than that of a traditional classroom. You should think of yourself as a facilitator rather than the teacher. The techniques you use from orienting your students, the observations of students, and the managing of the project need to allow students the space to produce their best work. This space is where students will navigate the risk section of learning and where the most effective lessons will occur.

The time directly after the project is finished is a crucial time where many lessons can be learned. You need to allow students to reflect upon their assessment, their collaboration, and lessons learned. If you simply start another project immediately after turning in the last one, life lessons and self-reflection might be lost.

Afterword

The single most important factor in determining America's success in the 21st century will be maintaining our ability to be an innovative and creative society.

—Ron Kind

CREATING THE 21ST CENTURY WORKER

The enGuage 21st Century Skills names four skill clusters essential to the 21st century workplace. They are the following:

- Digital-age literacy
- Invention thinking
- Effective communication
- High productivity (NCREL & Metri Group, 2003)

Within these skills are a subset of skills:

- Digital-age literacy
  - Technological literacy—understanding about technology and how it can be used
  - Information literacy—ability to find, access, and use information
  - Visual literacy—ability to understand, use, and create images and video using conventional and new media

- Inventive thinking
  - Adaptability and managing complexity—ability to deal with change positively
  - Self-direction—ability to work independently including setting goals and managing time as well as evaluating your own learning process

- o Risk taking—willingness to go beyond the safety zone and to make mistakes
- o Higher-order thinking—higher level thinking process including the ability to analyze, evaluate, and synthesize

- Effective communication
  - o Teaming and collaboration—a situation in which individuals share a common goal and the cooperative interaction between the members as they work together to achieve their goal
  - o Interactive communication—learning to communicate using a wide variety of media and technology
  - o Interpersonal skills—ability to manage one's behavior, emotions, and motivations to foster positive interactions with other individuals and groups

- High productivity
  - o Prioritizing, planning, and managing for results—organizational skills that help individuals achieve a goal through efficient management of time and resources
  - o Effective use of real-world tools—mastering current technology to communicate and collaborate with others to effectively problem solve
  - o Ability to produce relevant, high-quality products—ability to produce products that serve authentic purposes and occur as a result of using real-world tools (NCREL & Metri Group, 2003)

Ask yourself, do any of these sound familiar after reading what managing your classroom using PBL can provide for you and your students? Do not all of them sound familiar? By using project management to turn your classroom into a 21st century classroom, you are in effect creating 21st century workers who will have the necessary skills to succeed in the modern workplace. You are providing an advantage to your students that will enable them to be successful in whatever they set out to do.

PROJECT CONTRACT

Student(s) Name: _____

Project Topic: _____

Essential Question:

Due Date of Project:

Learning Outcomes *(at least three)*:

Group Goal(s): _____

_____

_____

Product of Project: _____

_____

_____

Student(s) Signature: _____

_____

_____

_____

Teacher Signature: _____

INTEROFFICE MEMORANDUM

FROM:

SUBJECT:

DATE:

PURPOSE

SUMMARY

DISCUSSION

RECOMMENDATION

PROJECT MANAGER

Goals	Major Tasks	Project Deadline	Responsible Party

Project Deadline: Day 1, Day 2, Day 3, Day 4, Day 5, Day 6, Day 7, Day 8, Day 9, Day 10, Day 11, Day 12, Day 13, Day 14

Responsible Party: Group member # 1, Group member # 2, Group member # 3, Group member # 4, Group member # 5

Goals: Goal # 1, Goal # 2, Goal # 3

COMPASS POINTS ACTIVITY DIRECTIONS

1. Describe for students that they will need to identify themselves as one of the four cardinal directions.
   - They may find themselves identifying with a couple of directions, but they have to find the one they most identify with, no intermediate directions

2. Read aloud the descriptions of each of the directions. Provide examples to clarify.

3. Once they have identified themselves, form groups in the four corners of the room, forming a compass rose of north, south, east, and west.

4. In those groups, take 5 minutes to answer the four questions. Have someone write the group responses down (can use chart paper to record).

5. Have someone in the group report out the group's answers to the questions.

6. Debrief about the activity and what each group learned about working with the other directions.

7. Summarize how highly successful groups would have people from all four directions. Having too many norths or too many easts in one group can cause problems.

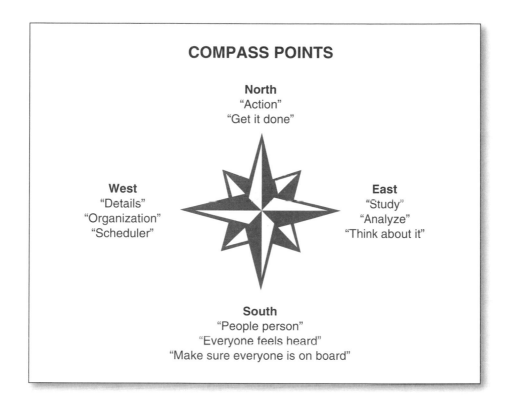

COMPASS POINTS

North
"Action"
"Get it done"

West
"Details"
"Organization"
"Scheduler"

East
"Study"
"Analyze"
"Think about it"

South
"People person"
"Everyone feels heard"
"Make sure everyone is on board"

COMPASS POINTS QUESTIONS

1) Use adjectives to describe strengths from your compass direction.

2) Use adjectives to describe weaknesses from your compass direction.

3) Which compass direction do you think you would work best with? Which would be the most challenging?

4) If your team did not have your compass direction, how do you think it would function?

PEER REVIEW OF WRITING

Reviewer: _____   Author: _____

Aspect evaluating	Grade					Comments
Introduction: Is the purpose of the paper clearly established?	A	B	C	D	F	
Use of Evidence: Does the author use reliable examples to back up statements made?	A	B	C	D	F	
Defense of thesis: Does the author make a sound argument throughout the paper?	A	B	C	D	F	
Mechanics. How is the spelling, punctuation, and sentence structure?	A	B	C	D	F	
Structure: Does the paper follow a clear five-part structure?	A	B	C	D	F	
Conclusion: Does the author summarize the main thesis of the paper and conclude it effectively?	A	B	C	D	F	
Bibliography: Does the author use proper formatting and have at least 10 references?	A	B	C	D	F	

INVENT A BETTER MOUSETRAP, AND THE WORLD WILL BEAT A PATH TO YOUR DOOR

Description

The above saying refers to the fact that if you improve upon an already existing product, you will become successful. Technology must always change to meet the needs of people. Could you imagine if we had never changed the original computer that was so large it took up an entire room? We are going to revisit a classic design of a product and try to improve upon it.

You will create a new mousetrap, one that captures the mouse without doing it harm unlike the original model. You will design the mousetrap first and then build a working model that will capture a stuffed mouse. Your design must include step by step how to create it, measurements, materials, and be detailed enough that if someone were to build the mousetrap using the design, they would be able to do so. You will also need to compare and contrast your mousetrap with the original one and evaluate that it is better and why.

Standard

Science 4–2: Revise an existing design used to solve a problem

Suggested Materials

Graph paper/drawing paper
Materials to build mousetrap

Timeline of Project

- Introduction to project/Review of old design: 1 day
- Design of trap: 2 days
- Construction of model: 3 days
- Presentation/Demonstration: 1 day

Products

- Design of your mousetrap
- Model of your mousetrap and demonstration of it
- Comparison between your mousetrap and the original

Sun	Mon	Tue	Wed	Thu	Fri	Sat

Student(s) _____ **Project** _____

Excellent (A)			
Good (B–C)			
Needs Improvement (D–F)			

Aspect of Project	Self _____	Peer _____	Peer _____

Aspect of Project	Peer _____	Peer _____	Peer _____

References

Arter, J., & McTighe, J. (2001). *Scoring rubrics in the classroom: Using performance criteria for assessing and improving student performance.* Thousand Oaks, CA: Corwin.

Auld, K. (2010). 5 tips to make your orientations successful! *BC Jobs Ca.* Retrieved from http://www.bcjobs.ca/hr-advice/5-tips-to-make-your-orientations-successful/

Benefits of public speaking for small business owners. (n.d.). IMpro Solutions: An Interactive Public Speaking System. Retrieved from http://www.impro solutions.com/benefits-of-public-speaking-for-small-business-owners/

Campbell, C. A. (2006). *The one-page project manager: Communicate and manage any project with a single sheet of paper.* Hoboken, NJ: Wiley.

Cobb, P., Wood, T., Yackel, E., Nicholls, J., Wheatley, G., Trigatti, B., & Perlwitz, M. (1991). Assessment of a problem-centered second-grade mathematics project. *Journal for Research in Mathematics Education, 22,* 3–29.

Common Core Correlation Guides. (2014). California Department of Resources Recycling and Recovery. Retrieved from http://www.californiaeei.org/curriculum/correlations/commoncore/

Costa, A. L., & Kalick, B. (2009). *Learning and leading with habits of mind.* Alexandria, VA: ASCD.

Darling-Hammond, L. (2013). *The flat world and education: How America's commitment to equity will determine our future.* New York, NY: Teachers College Press.

Framework for 21st Century Learning. (n.d.). Partnership for 21st Century Skills. Retrieved from http://www.p21.org/about-us/p21-framework

Goodrich, H. (1996). Understanding rubrics. *Educational Leadership, 54*(4), 14–18.

Great Schools Partnerships. (2013). Portfolio. The Glossary of Education Reform. Retrieved from http://edglossary.org/portfolio/

Hamel, G. (n.d.). The advantages to having a mission statement: Small business by Demand Media. Retrieved from http://smallbusiness.chron.com/advantages-having-mission-statement-17618.html

Harvard Business Schools Harvard Manage Mentor. (2007). Different types of presentations. Retrieved from http://sage.com.my/contents/demo_content/strategic_thinking/different_types_of_presentations.html

Heagney, J. (2012). *Fundamentals of project management* (4th ed.). New York, NY: American Management Association

Herman, J. L., Aschbacher, P. R., & Winters, L. (1992). *A practical guide to alternative assessment.* Alexandria, VA: ASCD.

Hewes, B. (2012). PBL: Project reflection questions. Retrieved from http://biancahewes.wordpress.com/2012/04/29/pbl-project-reflection-questions/

Human Resources—Common Rater Errors. (2014). Dartmouth College. Retrieved from http://www.dartmouth.edu/~hrs/profldev/performance_management/rater_errors.html

Institute of Education Sciences. Trends in International Mathematics and Sciences Study. U.S. Department of Education—National Center for Education Statistics. Retrieved from http://nces.ed.gov/timss/results11.asp

Jones, N. (2010). Collaboration at work: A look at the pros and cons. *Bright Hub.* Retrieved from http://www.brighthub.com/office/collaboration/articles/73856.aspx

Jones, R. D. (2006). *Introduction to Rigor/Relevance Framework.* Rexford, NY: International Center for Leadership in Education.

Karnes, F. A., & Riley, T. L. (2005). *Competitions for talented kids.* Waco, TX: Prufrock Press.

Lewis, J. P. (2006). *Fundamentals of project management* (3rd ed.). New York, NY: American Management Association

Lewis, P. (n.d.). What are the key steps for project management? *Ehow.* Retrieved from http://www.ehow.com/facts_4970073_what-key-steps-project-management.html

Mastering Project Management. (2014). *Project Closure—Whether your 1st or 21st project, successful completion involves a few important steps.* Retrieved from http://www.mastering-project-management.com/project-closure.html

McCain, T., & Jukes, I. (2001). *Windows on the future: Education in the age of technology.* Thousand Oaks, CA: Corwin.

National Engineers Week. (2011). What is Future City. Retrieved from http://futurecity.org/about

NCREL, & Metri Group. (2003). *enGauge 21st century skills: Literacy in the digital age.* Naperville, IL and Los Angeles, CA: NCREL & Metri.

Noble, C. (2013, April 1). First minutes are critical in new-employee orientation. *Forbes Magazine, 12*(8).

Oakley, B., Felder, R. M., Brent, R., & Elhajj, I. (2004). Turning student groups into effective teams. *Journal of Student Centered Learning, 2*(1), 9–34. Retrieved from http://www4.ncsu.edu/unity/lockers/users/f/felder/public/Papers/Oakley-paper(JSCL).pdf

Pennypaker, J. S. (1997). *Principles of project management.* Atlanta, GA: Project Management Institute Inc.

Richman, L. (2012). *Improving your project management skills.* New York, NY: American Management Association.

Ryan, R. M., & Grolnick, W. S. (1986). Origins and pawns in the classroom: Self-report and projective assessments of individual differences in children's perceptions. *Journal of Personality and Social Psychology, 50,* 550–558.

Stanley, T. (2011). *Project-based learning for gifted students: A handbook for the 21st-century classroom.* Waco, TX: Prufrock Press.

Stanley, T. (2014). *Performance-based assessment for 21st-century skills.* Waco, TX: Prufrock Press.

Stewart, J. (2012). Top 10 reasons why projects fail. Project-Management.com. Retrieved from http://project-management.com/top-10-reasons-why-projects-fail/

Thomas, J. W., Mergendoller, J. R., & Michaelson, A. (1999). *Project-based learning: A handbook for middle and high school teachers.* Novato, CA: The Buck Institute for Education.

Trends in International Mathematics and Science Study. (2011). National Center for Education Statistics. Retrieved from http://nces.ed.gov/timss/results11.asp

Trilling, B., & Fadel, C. (2009). *21st-century skills: Learning for life in our times.* Hoboken, NJ: Jossey-Bass.

Venn, J. J. (2000). *Assessing students with special needs* (2nd ed.). Upper Saddle River, NJ: Merrill.

Wagner, T. (2008) *The global achievement gap: Why even our best schools don't teach the new survival skills our children need—and what we can do about it.* New York, NY: Basic Books.

Wiggins, G., & McTighe, J. (2005). *Understanding by design.* Alexandria, VA: ASCD.

Index

CORWIN
A SAGE Company

Helping educators make the greatest impact

CORWIN HAS ONE MISSION: to enhance education through intentional professional learning.

We build long-term relationships with our authors, educators, clients, and associations who partner with us to develop and continuously improve the best evidence-based practices that establish and support lifelong learning.